Biblio. Deafness
Gary Austin, Ph.D.
Kenly's
815 David Ave.
DeKalb, Ill. 60115
3.50

Bill McCrone

EDUCATIONAL AND PSYCHOSOCIAL ASPECTS OF DEAFNESS

Publication No. 931

AMERICAN LECTURE SERIES

A Publication in
The BANNERSTONE DIVISION *of*
AMERICAN LECTURES IN SOCIAL AND REHABILITATION PSYCHOLOGY

Editors of the Series

JOHN G. CULL, PH.D.

Professor and Director, Regional Counselor Training Program
Department of Rehabilitation Counseling
Virginia Commonwealth University
Fishersville, Virginia

and

RICHARD E. HARDY, ED.D.

Professor and Chairman, Department of Rehabilitation Counseling
Virginia Commonwealth University
Richmond, Virginia

The American Lecture Series in Social and Rehabilitation Psychology offers books which are concerned with man's role in his milieu. Emphasis is placed on how this role can be made more effective in a time of social conflicts and deteriorating physical environment. The books are oriented toward descriptions of what future roles should be and are not concerned exclusively with the delineation and definition of contemporary behavior. Contributors are concerned to a considerable extent with prediction through the use of a functional view of man as opposed to a descriptive, anatomical point of view.

Books in this series are written mainly for the professional practitioner; however, academicians will find them of considerable value in both undergraduate and graduate courses in the helping services.

Educational and Psychosocial Aspects of Deafness

RICHARD E. HARDY

JOHN G. CULL

CHARLES C THOMAS · PUBLISHER

Springfield · Illinois · U.S.A.

Published and Distributed Throughout the World by
CHARLES C THOMAS • PUBLISHER
Bannerstone House
301-327 East Lawrence Avenue, Springfield, Illinois, U.S.A.

ISBN 0-398-03002-2
Library of Congress Catalog Card Number: 73 13901

With THOMAS BOOKS careful attention is given to all details of manufacturing and design. It is the Publisher's desire to present books that are satisfactory as to their physical qualities and artistic possibilities and appropriate for their particular use. THOMAS BOOKS will be true to those laws of quality that assure a good name and good will.

Printed in the United States of America
C-1

Library of Congress Cataloging in Publication Data

Hardy, Richard E.
Educational and psychosocial aspects of deafness.

(American lecture series, no. 931. A publication in the Bannerstone Division of American lectures in social and rehabilitation psychology)
1. Deaf—Education—United States—Addresses, essays, lectures. 2. Deaf—Rehabilitation—United States—Addresses, essays, lectures. 3. Deafness—Psychological aspects—Addresses, essays, lectures. I. Cull, John G., joint author. II. Title. [DNLM: 1. Deafness—Rehabilitation. HV2380 H271e 1974]

Library of Congress Cataloging in Publication Data

HV2545.H37 362.4'2'0973 73-13901
ISBN 0-398-03002-2

This book is dedicated to Mr. Boyce C. Williams for unusually innovative approaches in services to the deaf over many years as an outstanding leader in the field.

Other books appearing in the Social and Rehabilitation Psychology Series:

SOCIAL AND REHABILITATION SERVICES FOR THE BLIND
Richard E. Hardy and John G. Cull

DRUG DEPENDENCE AND REHABILITATION APPROACHES
Richard E. Hardy and John G. Cull

FUNDAMENTALS OF CRIMINAL BEHAVIOR AND CORRECTIONAL SYSTEMS
John G. Cull and Richard E. Hardy

VOLUNTEERISM: AN EMERGING PROFESSION
John G. Cull and Richard E. Hardy

APPLIED VOLUNTEERISM IN COMMUNITY DEVELOPMENT
Richard E. Hardy and John G. Cull

ADJUSTMENT TO WORK: A Goal of Rehabilitation
John G. Cull and Richard E. Hardy

SPECIAL PROBLEMS IN REHABILITATION
A. Beatrix Cobb

VOCATIONAL EVALUATION FOR REHABILITATION SERVICES
Richard E. Hardy and John G. Cull

THERAPEUTIC NEEDS OF THE FAMILY: Problems, Descriptions and Therapeutic Approaches
John G. Cull and Richard E. Hardy

CONTRIBUTORS

EDNA P. ADLER: Consultant, Deaf and the Hard of Hearing, Office of Deafness and Communicative Disorders, Department of Health, Education, and Welfare, Social and Rehabilitation Service, Washington, D. C.

BRIAN BOLTON, Ph.D.: Research Associate, Arkansas Rehabilitation Research and Training Center. He received his Ph.D. from the University of Wisconsin. Dr. Bolton is also Lecturer, Department of Psychology, University of Arkansas; Research Consultant, Children's House of Learning, El Dorado, Arkansas. Formerly, Assistant Professor of Psychology, Illinois Institute of Technology; Research Associate, Jewish Vocational Service, Chicago, Illinois. He is author of more than fifty publications in psychometrics, deafness and rehabilitation.

S. JAMES CUTLER, B.S.: Special Education, Temple University; M.S. in Rehabilitation Counseling, Virginia Commonwealth University. Mr. Cutler is Professor of Audiology, Department of Medicine, Medical College of Virginia, Health Sciences Division, Virginia Commonwealth University.

JOHN G. CULL, Ph.D.: Professor and Director, Regional Counselor Training Program, Department of Rehabilitation Counseling, Virginia Commonwealth University, Fishersville, Virginia; Adjunct Professor of Psychology and Education, School of General Studies, University of Virginia, Charlottesville, Virginia; Technical Consultant, Rehabilitation Services Administration, United States Department of Health, Education and Welfare, Washington, D. C.; Editor, *American Lecture Series in Social and Rehabilitation Psychology,* Charles C Thomas, Publisher; Lecturer Medical Department, Woodrow Wilson Rehabilitation Center; formerly, Rehabilitation Counselor, Texas State Commission for the Blind; Rehabilitation Counselor, Texas Rehabilitation Commission; Director, Division of Research and Program Development, Virginia State Department of Vocational Rehabilitation. The following are some of the books which Dr. Cull has co-authored and co-edited: *Drug Dependence and Rehabilitation Approaches, Fundamentals of Criminal Behavior and Correctional Systems, Rehabilitation of the Drug Abuser with Delinquent Behavior,* and *Therapeutic Needs of the Family.* Dr. Cull has contributed more than fifty publications to the professional literature in psychology and rehabilitation.

ANN GLASS: Rehabilitation Counselor for the Deaf for the Sacramento District, Sacramento, California. B.A.—University of California and M.A.—University of Oregon. Mrs. Glass has held positions as social worker and Field Work Supervisor, University of Oregon, Rehabilitation Counselor Training Program.

JOHN A. GRANT, M.D., M.P.H.: Deputy State Health Officer for Kent County, Maryland; Assistant Professor and Consultant in Community Pediatrics, Department of Pediatrics, University of Maryland School of Medicine, Baltimore, Maryland; Associate Department of Maternal and Child Health, School of Hygiene and Public Health, The Johns Hopkins University, Baltimore, Maryland. Formerly, Chief, School Health Section, Division of Maternal and Child Health, Maryland State Department of Health; Pediatric Consultant, Central Evaluation Clinic for Children, University of Maryland Hospital, Baltimore, Maryland. Editor, *Perspectives in Maternal and Child Health,* Department of Maternal and Child Health, School of Hygiene and Public Health, The Johns Hopkins University, Baltimore, Maryland. Doctor Grant has contributed extensively to the professional literature in screening technology and program evaluation in pediatrics and public health.

RICHARD E. HARDY, Ed.D.: Professor and Chairman, Department of Rehabilitation Counseling, Virginia Commonwealth University, Richmond, Virginia; Technical Consultant, United States Department of Health, Education and Welfare, Rehabilitation Services Administration, Washington, D. C.; Editor, *American Lecture Series in Social and Rehabilitation Psychology,* Charles C

Thomas, Publisher; and Associate Editor, *Journal of Voluntary Action Research;* formerly Rehabilitation Counselor in Virginia; Rehabilitation Advisor, Rehabilitation Services Administration, United States Department of Health, Education and Welfare, Washington, D. C.; former Chief Psychologist and Supervisor of Professional Training, South Carolina Department of Rehabilitation and member of the South Carolina State Board of Examiners in Psychology. The following are some of the books which Dr. Hardy has co-authored and co-edited: *Drug Dependence and Rehabilitation Approaches, Fundamentals of Criminal Behavior and Correctional Systems, Rehabilitation of the Drug Abuser with Delinquent Behavior,* and *Therapeutic Needs of the Family.* Dr. Hardy has contributed more than fifty publications to the professional literature in psychology and rehabilitation.

HELEN SCHICK LANE, Ph.D.: Psychologist and Consultant, Central Institute for the Deaf; Professor of Education, Graduate Institute of Education, Washington University (St. Louis). Formerly Principal of Central Institute for the Deaf (1941-72); Associate Professor of Psychology, Washington University (1941-61); President of the A. G. Bell Association for the Deaf (1965-69). Doctor Lane has contributed to the professional literature in the field of psychology of the deaf, especially in the application of mental and educational achievement tests to deaf children.

ROBERT O. LANKENAU: Supervisor, Chemical Laboratories, Firestone Tire and Rubber Company, Akron, Ohio; Immediate Past President, National Association of the Deaf; Former Member, National Advisory Committee on the Education of the Deaf; Member, Governor's Committee on the Employment of the Handicapped; Member, President's Committee on Employment of the Handicapped; Member of the Board and Chairman, Teletype Committee, National Association of the Deaf; Member, Professional Advisory Board, Comprehensive Services for the Deaf, Akron University; Member, Registry of Interpreters for the Deaf; Member, Evaluation Committee for Ohio Interpreters for the Deaf.

CARL A. LARSON, M.D.: Instructor, Medical Genetics, University of Lund, Staff Physician, Research Department, St. Lars Hospital, Lund, Sweden.

ROBERT A. LASSITER, Ph.D.: Assistant Professor, Department of Rehabilitation Counseling, School of Community Services, Virginia Commonwealth University; Technical Consultant, Rehabilitation Services Administration, Department of Health, Education and Welfare; Contributor, American Lecture Series in Social and Rehabilitation Psychology, Charles C Thomas, Publisher. Formerly, Chairman, Rehabilitation Counseling Program, School of Education, University of North Carolina at Chapel Hill; State Director of Vocational Rehabilitation in North Carolina; Executive Director, North Carolina Society for Crippled Children and Adults; Rehabilitation Counselor and Supervisor in the Florida Vocational Rehabilitation program. Doctor Lassiter is the author of articles in various professional publications.

STEPHEN P. QUIGLEY, Ph.D.: Professor of Education and of Speech and Hearing Science in the Institute for Research on Exceptional Children at the University of Illinois at Urbana-Champaign. Doctor Quigley received an A.B. degree in Psychology from the University of Denver, an M.A. degree in Speech and Hearing Disorders from the University of Illinois and a Ph.D. degree in Speech Science from the University of Illinois. Doctor Quigley was a Ford Foundation Post-Doctoral Fellow at the Institute for Research on Exceptional Children, University of Illinois and concurrently trained as a teacher of deaf children at the Illinois School for the Deaf. Formerly, Professor of Psychology and Director of the Office of Psycho-Educational Research at Gallaudet College. He also served as editor of *dsh Abstracts;* Executive Secretary of the Sensory Disabilities Study Section of the United States Office of Vocational Rehabilitation; on the faculty and served as Acting Director of the Institute for Research on Exceptional Children at the University of Illinois. Doctor Quigley is currently directing a large scale investigation of the acquisition of language by deaf children and a study of evaluation techniques for interpreters for deaf people.

PAUL ROTTER, Ed.D.: Lexington School for the Deaf. Doctor Rotter obtained a B.S. in Special Education from Columbia University, M.A. in Education of the Deaf, Columbia University and Ed.D. in Education and Administration of the Deaf, Columbia University. Doctor Rotter is certified in New York State as teacher of the deaf and hard of hearing; principal, elementary school, principal, secondary school. Formerly, Supervisor of Upper School and High School for the deaf, Assistant to the Superintendent, Assistant Superintendent, Director of Pupil Personnel, and Director of Buildings and Grounds. Doctor Rotter has published extensively in all aspects of deafness.

BOYCE R. WILLIAMS: Director, Office of Deafness and Communicative Disorders, Rehabilitation Services Administration, United States Department of Health, Education and Welfare, Washington, D. C. Mr. Williams received an M.A. degree from Columbia University in 1940. Formerly, Teacher at the Wisconsin School for the Deaf, High School teacher and Vocational Training Director, Indiana School for the Deaf; Consultant for the Deaf, the Hard of Hearing, and the Speech Impaired, Rehabilitation Services Administration, United States Department of Health, Education and Welfare. Mr. Williams is associated with many professional associations pertaining to the deaf.

PREFACE

THE DEVELOPMENT of this book has been most difficult in that the persons who were carefully selected to contribute are most outstanding and also heavily over-burdened in their professional involvements. It has, however, been well worth the effort in that we are delighted with the book in terms of the contribution we feel it will make.

We stressed over and over to our contributors that we wanted the text to be practitioner oriented, pragmatic, realistic, *down to earth,* and to have as few as possible of the philosophic platitudes and academic cliches that are generally found in many textbooks. This book stems from not only our interest in the field of rehabilitation and its broad aspects as this concerns the deaf population but also the expressed need of many rehabilitation counselors, psychologists, social workers and other professional persons who were most concerned about available practitioner oriented materials.

We would like to acknowledge our debt to Margie Alexy for her invaluable editorial and clerical assistance; not only in the development of this book but in the development of all books in the Social and Rehabilitation Psychology Series.

RICHARD E. HARDY
JOHN G. CULL

Richmond, Virginia

CONTENTS

EDUCATIONAL AND PSYCHOSOCIAL ASPECTS OF DEAFNESS

Chapter I

SERVICES TO DEAF PEOPLE IN THE SEVENTIES

EDNA P. ADLER AND BOYCE R. WILLIAMS

Education
Vocational Rehabilitation
Community Development
Service Delivery
Services for Parents of Preschool Age Deaf Children
Mental Health Centers for Deaf People
Rehabilitation Centers for Deaf Individuals
Telecommunication for the Deaf
Manual Communication Development

I. CURRENT CIRCUMSTANCES

Population Analysis and Description

APPROXIMATELY FIVE PERCENT of the total population in this country are persons handicapped by a significant bilateral hearing loss. About two million of them cannot hear and understand conversational speech. The ongoing National Census of the Deaf Population which defines a deaf person as one who has lost, or never had, the ability to hear and understand speech through the unaided ear, such loss to have occurred prior to nineteen years of age, tentatively reports a prevalence rate for deafness of two per one thousand. It is estimated there are over 450,000 individuals who fit into this category. The figure does not include institutionalized deaf persons (Schein, 1972).

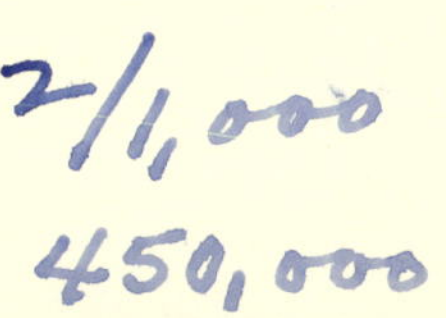

Most young deaf people today were either born without hearing or lost it soon after birth. This is in marked contrast to twenty-five or thirty years ago when the majority of deaf persons began life with normal hearing, losing it later as the result of the then prevailing contagious diseases, spinal meningitis, scarlet fever, measles, and others. Congenital deafness due to heredity and other causes such as maternal rubella, Rh factor, and prematurity, and early deafness brought on by complications attending birth or occurring soon after birth form the main etiology of severe or total hearing impairment today. Presbycusia, which refers to the gradual loss of hearing over a period of time, is commonly found in aging persons.

Individuals in whom deafness occurred before basic language and speech patterns were developed are frequently referred to as the prelingually deafened. Those who become deaf after the age of four or five and later, when communication patterns are normally well established, are termed postlingually or adventitiously deafened. By far, the population of younger deaf people today who will be the rehabilitation clients of tomorrow are characterized by prelingual deafness due to the fact that most of them were either born deaf or lost their hearing before the age of three or four.

Deafness is largely irreversible and does not normally respond to surgery, medication or instrumentation such as hearing aids. It is in the main a communication problem, accompanied by psychosocial difficulties that vary in severity from individual to individual depending on such factors as age at onset of deafness, the presence of other handicapping conditions, and the availability of timely, appropriate and adequate training and adjustment services.

The well-adjusted deaf person with good communication skills may regard his hearing deprivation as merely an inconvenience in meeting the demands of daily living. However, at such times, for example, as when he urgently needs to make a telephone call or receive emergency information being relayed on television, he is apt to appreciate the severity of his handicap. For a great many deaf people on the other hand, communication is a far more serious problem affecting all phases and stages of their lives. In spite of the normal strength, intelligence and mobility that most deaf persons have, limited communication skills such as inadequate speech and poor reading and writing abilities deprive them of opportunity to engage in activities whereby they might better realize their personal, social and occupational potential.

In essence, the handicaps of deafness are psychosocial, manifesting themselves, in many cases, in severe underdevelopment of the person, social isolation and unemployment or underemployment. Partially counteracting this is the unique stronghold of the organized deaf community with its network of social and athletic clubs and churches where manual communication is supreme and meets the needs of countless deaf people for information outlets and personal succor in the forms of satisfying companionship and ego satisfaction.

Education

The number of school age deaf children is estimated to be close to 90,000 with 5,000 at the kindergarten level, 56,000 at the elementary level and 28,000 at the secondary level. A 1971 survey of schools and classes for the deaf placed the number of deaf children in attendance at 46,075. It is believed that there are ten to fifteen thousand additional unreported children attending itinerant and other programs. In addition, approximately two thousand deaf adults are enrolled at special postsecondary programs established to meet their higher education, vocational-technical training and comprehensive rehabilitation needs. An unknown number attend adult education programs in the few communities that provide this service to deaf people and others with or without the help of interpreters attend programs for the normally hearing up to and including the doctoral level (Schein, 1972).

The latest report available in 1971 reveals that a total of 674 schools and classes were providing educational services to deaf children ranging from preschool to high school level training. The sixty-one public residential schools in operation had the largest enrollment serving 18,767 deaf children. Public day classes with a total of 413 units had the next largest enrollment, 16,235, followed by fifty-five public day schools serving 5,784 deaf children, twelve private residential schools with 1,874 pupils, thirty-one private day schools with 1,174 pupils, fifty-two multi-handicapped classes serving 1,242, and fifty private day classes having 1,026 students.

Approximately three thousand deaf children are graduated or terminate their attendance at these programs annually. Available post-secondary training opportunities for deaf youth and adults include two degree granting programs in the eastern part of the country, Gallaudet College in Washington, D. C. and the National Technical Institute for the Deaf in Rochester, New York and one on the west coast at California State University in Northridge. A phenomenon of recent years that has provided

TABLE I-I

POST-SECONDARY TRAINING PROGRAMS FOR DEAF STUDENTS, 1972

Program
Gallaudet College, Washington, D. C.
National Technical Institute for the Deaf, Rochester, New York
Golden West College, Huntington Beach, California
California State University at Northridge, Northridge, California
St. Paul Technical Vocational Institute, St. Paul, Minnesota
Seattle Community College, Seattle, Washington
La Puente Valley Vocational Adult School, City of Industry, California
Community College of Denver, Denver, Colorado
Delgado Vocational Technical Junior College, New Orleans, Louisiana
Lee College, Baytown, Texas
State Technical Institute and Rehabilitation Center, Plainwell, Michigan
Northern Illinois University, De Kalb, Illinois
San Diego Community Colleges, San Diego, California
Johnson County Community College, Overland Park, Kansas
Ohlone College, Freemont, California
Riverside City College, Riverside, California
St. Petersburg Junior College, Clearwater Campus, Clearwater, Florida
Columbus Technical Institute, Columbus, Ohio
Eastfield College, Mesquite, Texas
Jefferson County Area Vocational School, Jeffersontown, Kentucky
Genesee Community College, Flint, Michigan
Iowa Western Community College, Council Bluffs, Iowa
Tennessee Temple Schools, Chattanooga, Tennessee
Pasadena City College, Pasadena, California
Tarrant County Junior College, Hurst, Texas
Community College of Philadelphia, Philadelphia, Pennsylvania
Hyles-Anderson College, Hammond, Indiana

TABLE I-II

REHABILITATION PROGRAMS SERVING DEAF PEOPLE, 1972

Alabama Institute for Deaf and Blind, Talladega, Alabama
University of Arizona Rehabilitation Center, Tucson, Arizona
Project with Multi-Handicapped Deaf Adults, Hot Springs Rehabilitation Center, Hot Springs, Arkansas
Graham H. Anthony Vocational Rehabilitation Center, American School for the Deaf, West Hartford, Connecticut
Vocational Rehabilitation Program, Florida School for the Deaf, St. Augustine, Florida
Evaluation Center for the Deaf, Cave Spring, Georgia
Community Project for the Deaf, Jewish Vocational Service, Chicago, Illinois
Crossroads Rehabilitation Center, Inc., Indianapolis, Indiana
Rehabilitation Center, Delgado College, New Orleans, Louisiana
State Technical Institute and Rehabilitation Center, Deaf Services Department, Plainwell, Michigan
Rehabilitation Center and Workshop of Greater St. Paul, Inc., St. Paul, Minnesota
Jewish Employment and Vocational Service, Work Experience Center Program, St. Louis, Missouri
New York Society for the Deaf Prevocational, Evaluation and Training Center, New York, New York
Vocational Rehabilitation Center, North Carolina School for the Deaf, Morganton, North Carolina
Comprehensive Program for the Deaf, Hearing and Speech Center of Columbus and Central Ohio, Columbus, Ohio
Pennsylvania Rehabilitation Center, Johnstown, Pennsylvania
Vocational Rehabilitation Center of Allegheny County, Pittsburgh, Pennsylvania
Program for the Deaf, Chattanooga-Hamilton County Speech and Hearing Center, Chattanooga, Tennessee
Woodrow Wilson Rehabilitation Center, Fishersville, Virginia
Program for the Deaf, Seattle Hearing and Speech Center, Seattle, Washington
West Virginia Rehabilitation Center and Workshop, Institute, West Virginia
Wisconsin Rehabilitation Center for the Deaf, Delavan, Wisconsin

deaf people with urgently needed choices in post-secondary training opportunities is rapid increase to a total now greater than twenty-five in vocational-technical programs at community colleges that serve deaf individuals through systems that provide both integrated and segregated coursework with special assistance supplied by coordinators, tutors, counselors and interpreters. Table I-I presents a list of the post-secondary training programs that were available to deaf adults in 1972 (Stuckless & Delgado, 1973).

There are about twenty rehabilitation programs for deaf adults in various parts of the country, some of which provide diagnostic, evaluation and adjustment services to secondary school age deaf children as well. The list in Table I-II identifies these programs.

The United States Office of Education, Bureau of Education for the Handicapped, which was established in 1967, provides consultation and other assistance to state special education services, administers and carries out programs and projects for the training of teachers of the handicapped, and manages an extensive program of research in special education and training. The educational needs of deaf people are a part of this work. The Bureau also is involved in the production and distribution of instructional and other media, along with research and training specific to media to promote the educational advancement of deaf people. Through its Media Services and Captioned Films Branch, the Bureau provides a free loan service of educational and cultural media to deaf persons, parents of deaf children and other persons directly involved in work for the advancement of deaf people.

In 1970, Gallaudet College was authorized through an act of Congress to establish a Center for Continuing Education. The Center is conducting a community program in continuing education for deaf people residing in Metropolitan Washington to serve as a model for other communities.

Vocational Rehabilitation

It is estimated that on any given day of the year over seventeen thousand deaf persons are receiving services provided through the State-Federal vocational rehabilitation program with approximately 7,500 being rehabilitated annually. This is in sharp contrast to the 1950's when as many as five thousand deaf persons might have been found in service status with the annual total of deaf rehabilitations in the neighborhood of 2,500.

The Vocational Rehabilitation Act of 1954 which authorized a comprehensive research and training grant program was largely responsible for the substantial increase in numbers of deaf rehabilitants beginning in the 1960's. Through research, service techniques needed by deaf people have been and continue to be developed, refined and demonstrated aiding immeasurably in their rehabilitation. For example, a freestanding project for very severely handicapped deaf males which demonstrated in the early 1960's their feasibility for rehabilitation services and employment was the forerunner of the Regional Centers for Deaf Individuals which would be authorized in legislation that Congress has twice approved.

The concept of coordinating, referral, and supportive counseling services for deaf people so that they will be both aware of and able to secure their rights in public and other services is another demonstration of great impact. It has already provided substantial guidance to many communities over the country and will continue to be a basic point of reference for many years to come.

Following the specific authorization of interpreting, as a rehabilitation case service to deaf people through Public Law 89-433 in 1965, the successful establishment of the Registry of Interpreters for the Deaf as a Social and Rehabilitation Service demonstration project has resulted in vastly increased recruitment of interpreters needed by deaf people in daily activities, by the state vocational rehabilitation agencies and by other agencies and programs serving deaf persons.

Research and demonstration projects have made it possible to study emotional disturbance in deaf people and to develop appropriate mental health service techniques for them. They have also led to in-service training about deafness and skill in communicating for psychiatrists, social workers, psychologists, nurses, and counselors. Through research and demonstration pioneering, permanent inpatient and outpatient mental health programs have come into being to restore long hospitalized deaf individuals to the community and to prevent and reduce serious and incipient mental illness in others through early intervention.

Short term training programs have been an important means for development and extension of the capability of the State-Federal vocational rehabilitation program to serve deaf persons. Standards and guidelines for case services to deaf people have been developed through workshops of professionals and consumers. Technical procedures such as psychological testing of and interpreting to deaf people have been defined and standardized through the workshop tool. Likewise, orientation to the rehabilitation of deaf people has been provided to religious workers, social workers, psychologists and educators serving the deaf. Workshops have also been invaluable for training deaf leadership for the critical responsibility of active roles in community development. Moreover, specific organizational and institutional developments to provide for the responsiveness and focus that underpin and reinforce community capacity to meet the needs of special populations have their origins in workshops. The National Technical Institute for the Deaf, the Professional Rehabilitation Workers With the Adult Deaf, the Council of Organizations Serving the Deaf, and the Registry of Interpreters for the Deaf are cases in point. The identification and formalization of basic criteria for the development and operation of facilities for the deaf are also products of the short term training authorization.

Innovation and expansion grants to state vocational rehabilitation agencies and to other public and private agencies have made it possible for them to increase their capacity and capability to serve deaf people. Project D.E.A.F. (Diagnosis, Evaluation and Adjustment of the Deaf) in Columbus, Ohio, which was established as an expansion project to increase the number of deaf persons rehabilitated annually is now operated by the state, enabling increasing numbers of deaf individuals to receive the services they need to achieve their employment potential. Innovation projects have provided adjustment services during the summer months to deaf youth still in secondary programs readying them for formal rehabilitation services upon completion of school.

Community Development

Improvement in the circumstances of deaf people requires a responsive deaf community and effective deaf leadership. National and regional workshops to train deaf leadership in community development and organization have netted substantial results. More such workshops are needed. The National Association of the Deaf, an organization operated by and for deaf people, is the principal spokesman and advocate for the deaf consumer and carries the major responsibility in developing the national deaf community. In sponsoring national, regional, state, and local programs that are elevating the level of services available to deaf people, it is concurrently increasing public awareness of and responsiveness to the needs of deaf people. The organization which maintains offices at Halex House, 814 Thayer Avenue, Silver Spring, Maryland 20910, publishes *The Deaf American,* a monthly journal directed to the deaf consumer, parents of deaf people and professionals.

The Council of Organizations Serving the Deaf, an umbrella agency of organizations of and for the deaf established in 1968, serves as a sounding board and backstop for the deaf community and provides the means, mainly through its function as an information center and at annual forums, for the dissemination of knowledge about deafness and deaf people that would not otherwise be available to the public.

The Registry of Interpreters for the Deaf maintains a national registry of professional interpreters, assists in the development and operation of state chapters and promotes the certification and training of interpreters.

The Professional Rehabilitation Workers with the Adult Deaf, a voluntary organization of rehabilitation personnel, educators, social workers, psychologists, psychiatrists, guidance counselors, religious workers, hearing aid dealers, audiologists, speech pathologists and others serving deaf adults established in 1966, provides needed opportunity to cross disciplinary lines to share information and knowledge about deafness on behalf of a population for whom effective professionals are too few and widely scattered geographically. The organization maintains a national office in Washington, D. C. and issues a quarterly journal, a newsletter and an annual *Deafness* publication which documents federally supported research and training projects in the area of deafness and reports on trends. Biennial conferences are sponsored where special interest groups have the opportunity to meet and discuss pertinent needs and problems in their areas. Inquiries concerning membership and subscriptions may be addressed to PRWAD, 814 Thayer Avenue, Silver Spring, Maryland 20910.

Service Delivery

The shortage of trained manpower in the area of service to deaf people is a persistent and pervasive problem. There are approximately 1,500 interpreters available to serve deaf people, the majority of whom have received no formal training for the exacting work that they perform. They are largely the sons and daughters of deaf parents, religious workers and other persons with acquired manual communication skills who are helping to meet the rapidly growing demand for interpreters in the area of vocational rehabilitation, at the increasing number of post-secondary programs for the deaf, at secondary programs for the normally hearing attended by deaf students, at mental health facilities, in courtrooms and at community service agencies. The effectiveness of professional training in preparing interpreters for either full or part time work with deaf people in the various settings where they are needed has been well proved at the few available training resources, such as the Deafness Research and Training Center at New York University and the California State University at Northridge, and in the outstanding services resulting.

A severe shortage of clinical and consulting psychologists trained to work with deaf people continues to impede rehabilitation program development and to reduce the effectiveness of ongoing programs where their availability can spell the difference between successful and unsuccessful rehabilitation outcome for deaf persons. Mental health programs, rehabilitation resources and community centers serving deaf people, educational programs for deaf children, and higher education and vocational training programs for deaf adults need the services of psychologists who are uniquely positioned to contribute to program development in addition to their critically needed services to individual deaf persons. Basic requirements for psychologists working with deaf people in addition to graduate level training in their specializations include orientation to deafness, supervised practical experience in working with deaf people and facility in the use of manual communication.

Psychiatric service is available to deaf people in only a few communities and most hospitalized deaf persons receive minimal if any psychiatric treatment due to the communication problems involved. The small number, probably fewer than a dozen, of psychiatrists who have the necessary communication skills and knowledge about deafness to serve mentally ill and emotionally disturbed deaf persons adequately is not expected to grow significantly at the present time. Over the years it may be anticipated that as more ongoing successful programs and practitioners gain visibility in professional circles and in media, state and local interests will join forces to mount mental health programs for deaf people. On the same basis, an increasing number of psychiatrists will gradually be attracted to the specialty of deafness.

At the present time, interpreters trained to work in psychiatric settings are urgently needed. Their availability would do much to provide needed momentum in improving and increasing mental health services to deaf individuals. Known locations where inpatient and outpatient mental health service is currently available to deaf people include the New York State Psychiatric Institute with its Rockland State Hospital unit and Maimonides Hospital in greater New York City, Dixmont Hospital in Pittsburgh, Saint Elizabeth's Hospital in Washington, D. C., Michael Reese Hospital in Chicago, Austin State Hospital, Austin, Texas and Langley Porter Neuropsychiatric Institute, San Francisco. In addition, New York City, Washington and Austin have halfway houses that assist the former deaf mental patient in his return to the community.

Social workers with the special skills and knowledge needed for work with deaf people are in extremely short supply. Most of those who are available may be found at elementary residential schools, mental health facilities, community service centers and post-secondary programs for the deaf. An undergraduate program in social work established at Gallaudet College in 1970 is stimulating increasing numbers of deaf students to prepare for careers in social service work with deaf people, an area for which they have special aptitude and deep personal interest and commitment. A graduate level program in social work in the area of the deaf at Western Maryland College promises to increase further the number of available trained social workers. Other promising programs, now in the development stage, which propose to train undergraduates and graduates in vocational rehabilitation counseling to and social work for the deaf in a common setting for improved interdisciplinary action between these two interdependent fields will contribute additional valuable workers.

Most state vocational rehabilitation agencies now have at least one counselor trained to serve deaf people. In the larger and more heavily populated states, each region or metropolitan area may have a counselor working full or part time with deaf clients. Close to half of the states currently hire coordinators who, along with supervisory responsibilities, work to develop their statewide programs for deaf people including planning and developing needed resources.

At the present time, approximately 175 rehabilitation counselors are working exclusively with deaf people or serve mixed caseloads of deaf and hearing people. The majority of them are stationed at state rehabilitation agency district offices with others serving at rehabilitation programs located at the state residential schools for the deaf, at post-secondary programs and at mental health facilities. Six long term training programs in deafness rehabilitation are turning out annually approximately sixty counselors trained to work with deaf people. It has been estimated that at least twice that many are needed each year to meet the manpower needs of ongoing and developing programs. There is an immediate need for the establishment of one long term training program in deafness rehabilitation in each of the ten social and rehabilitation service regions. Presently, only five of the regions have a program with Region IX having two. Table I-III provides definitive information about the six ongoing programs.

Skilled evaluators to work with deaf people at diagnostic, evaluation, and work adjustment centers are also in short supply. Their services are especially critical to the deaf person interested in achieving maximum employment utilizing intrinsic skills and to the severely handicapped deaf individual who needs intensive

TABLE I-III

LONG-TERM TRAINING PROGRAMS IN REHABILITATION OF THE DEAF, 1973

Sponsoring Institution	*Program Title and Description*	*Program Level*
New York University	Deafness Research and Training Center (RT-17) arranges an appropriate program of study within the University combining professional education with special preparation for work with deaf vocational rehabilitation clients.	Master's Specialist Certificate Doctoral
University of Pittsburgh Pittsburgh, Pennsylvania 15213	Rehabilitation of the Deaf Individuals entering the program already possess professional competencies in such fields as rehabilitation counseling, audiology, education, and psychology. Training provides such professionals with the necessary knowledge, understanding and communication skills for meeting the needs of deaf people.	Master's Specialist Certificate Doctoral
University of Tennessee Department of Special Education and Rehabilitation Knoxville, Tennessee 37916	Rehabilitation Counselor Training This is a twelve week course that provides orientation to the nature of deafness, its impact on the individual and needs of deaf people.	Orientation
University of Arizona College of Education Tucson, Arizona 85721	Rehabilitation Counseling for the Deaf Training Program The program provides a background of several different counseling theories and techniques and opportunity for practicum.	Master's Doctoral
Oregon College of Education Monmouth, Oregon 97361	Program in Counseling the Deaf A four week course, the program provides orientation to the needs and problems of profoundly deaf adults.	Orientation
California State University College of Education Northridge, California 91324	Leadership Training Program in the Area of the Deaf This is a two semester program designed to provide special school and public administration training for persons experienced in working with deaf people.	Master's

and extensive assistance in preparing for employment or for possible vocational training.

II. THE PROMISE OF THE SEVENTIES

Services for Parents of Preschool Age Deaf Children

Services to deaf people in the seventies will need to focus sharply on the home environment of deaf children, particularly the preschool age deaf child and his parents who continue to be relatively unserved. Better methods for early diagnosis of deafness are a pressing need. Too many deaf children continue to remain unidentified and unserved due to the lack of refined instruments needed for detection of hearing loss in the very young and the general poor understanding of the disability of deafness. It is characteristic that most parents of deaf babies will suspect deafness but may receive a negative reaction from doctors who too often advise waiting for indications that the symptoms of slow communication development will disappear as the child grows.

Valuable time is thus lost when medical intervention might correct the deafness or early fitting with a hearing aid and communication training might begin to alleviate the serious effects of partial or total deafness engendered at birth or soon after. The parent, too, needs early help in adjusting to the fact of deafness which not infrequently precipitates serious psychological problems within the family further depriving the young deaf child of the supportive environment he needs.

Authorities on early childhood deafness such as Eugene Mindel, McCay Vernon, Hilde Schlesinger and Kay Meadow stress the importance of early detection and acceptance of deafness, and availability of information for parents so that they may acquire a realistic attitude toward the disability and be supported in their efforts in providing appropriate home training for their deaf child. Total communication, meaning the simultaneous use of gestures, speech, lipreading, amplification, writing, sign language and finger spelling in whatever combinations are effective in given situations or with a particular deaf child is strongly endorsed by these authorities in the need to establish early normal social interaction between the deaf child, his hearing family and the rest of his milieu.

Program needs in the area of preschool age deaf children cluster around diagnostic and information centers where parents may obtain accurate evaluation of deafness and guidance on available services such as home visitations by social workers with special training in early deafness, community programs for preschool deaf children and their parents, information about local, state and national organizations and agencies concerned with deafness and literature on deafness and deaf people. An especially urgent need that could be met in the seventies is the establishment of a strong national organization crystallizing the interests of all parents of deaf children into active state and local chapters where parents of preschool age deaf children could obtain needed information, guidance, and specific help.

Mental Health Centers for Deaf People

Presently, there are only three state mental health programs for deaf people, and one national program with limited intake, none of which are staffed to serve deaf children. This sorry situation exists in the face of research findings that indicate a higher incidence of emotional disturbance in the deaf population than in the general population. Part of the problem has been the scarcity of mental health personnel including psychiatrists, psychiatric social workers, psychologists, and nurses trained to work with deaf people. While it is customary for hospitalized, normally hearing persons to be restored early to the community, deaf patients are apt to languish for months and years in hospitals where their needs remain unmet. A large scale training program on mental health services to the deaf and severely hearing impaired for personnel in psychiatry is a top priority need in the seventies to increase sharply the availability and effectiveness of ongoing service programs. It should include university courses in orientation to deafness, in-service training arrangements, practicum under supervision of the known experts in extending mental health services to deaf persons, intensive training in manual communication, and a special mission to recruit more workers into this personnel starved field (Rainer and Altshuler, 1970).

Coordination, Evaluation, Referral and Counseling Centers

Communities that have established service centers for deaf people find without exception that regular service agencies as well as deaf persons are quick to respond to the services that the centers are in a position to offer. Due to the communication problems involved, many deaf people are unable to utilize the services that are normally available through service agencies despite the interest of the latter in assisting them. As a consequence, they are deprived of numerous community services that normally hearing persons take for granted. The Pittsburgh Counseling Center for the Deaf is an excellent example of deaf community development that follows when coordinating, referral, evaluation and counseling services are made available to deaf individuals and agencies that wish to serve them. In addition to routine services which include provision of interpreting services to agencies with deaf clients, diagnostic and evaluation services for deaf clients of the Pennsylvania Bureau of Vocational Rehabilitation, direct counseling for deaf persons and their families, employment placement and conducting an adult education program, the Center identified other community needs and helped meet them in aiding the development of an effective service for deaf persons in an ongoing vocational rehabilitation center and an in-hospital mental health center for deaf patients. Other community service programs for the deaf are operating in Seattle, Kansas City, Akron, New York City, Detroit and Dallas. Many more are needed and should materialize in many metropolitan areas in the seventies as the effectiveness of the ongoing programs becomes known and is related by program developers to the needs of deaf people in their own communities.

Rehabilitation Centers for Deaf Individuals

The Rehabilitation Acts of 1972 and 1973 include authorization for rehabilitation centers for deaf individuals to make it possible for those deaf persons who cannot be served at existing facilities to obtain the intensive diagnostic and training services that they need in order to achieve economic and social independence. The population to be served includes deaf individuals sixteen years of age and over who, due to communication and language deficiencies, poor social adjustment, inadequate vocational and academic skills, additional physical disabilities and emotional and other behavioral problems, have been unable to obtain in existing resources the kind of training and services they need to become employable. The establishment and operation of at least a model center of this kind in the seventies is very much a top priority in program development in the deaf area. The training of personnel to work with severely handicapped deaf adults, the development of effective training techniques and materials, with special attention to appropriate media and software, and research into the prevention and amelioration and adjustment to the multiple handicaps of deaf people will be a prime target effort.

Telecommunication for the Deaf

Prominent in this recent legislation is a new category of vocational rehabilitation service, *telecommunications, sensory, and other technological aids and devices.* This authorization reflects the growing awareness among professional and consumer leadership that instrumentation on behalf of disabled people has been inadequately exploited. Particularly significant for deaf people is the development of community systems of telecommunication utilizing over regular telephone wires teletypewriters, electrowriters, specially equipped television sets, and speech indicators. With this electronic innovation, the deaf person's involvement is at once expanded so greatly as to nullify in important aspects the rigid containment of personal goals that have been observed too frequently among the deaf population. The telephone has been a persistent obstacle to deaf job seekers, especially in the professions and other high level employment. While an important start has already been made in this direction, much remains to be done. Early evidence of improvement in level of job placement for deaf clients should materialize as instruments are used in the vocational rehabilitation process to train and place deaf people.

The relevancy of these exciting developments and prospects to better life experience for deaf persons is apparent with reflection upon the growing number of teletype equipped answering services that provide deaf teletype owners with normal access to emergency services, commercial establishments, other public services, church, and any interest that people routinely reach by telephone. The day is at hand when a deaf family will no longer need to depend upon neighbors to call the fire department or the doctor. As telecommunication spreads, deaf people will be able to order merchandise by telephone as do others, to check the time and the weather, to inquire about or initiate a personal, social or cultural project without needing to drive many miles for face to face discussion or to depend upon mail.

Important momentum is generating growing concern that television attend more to its visual output in providing hearing impaired viewers reasonable opportunity to understand and share programs. The Council of Organizations Serving the Deaf and its member organizations have generated government awareness of and interest in the need to explain on TV screens through easily understood symbols what emergency exists. Consequently, a growing number of emergency announcements now provide more than the aural cues.

The brighter day in prospect for deaf people assumes more substance with knowledge that the National Bureau of Standards has developed a module that will permit captions of simultaneous captioning of telecast programs. More and more local stations are using sign interpreters with newscasts by split screen, cameo, and other techinques. Important public interest programs have been taped and re-telecast with running captions at the base of the picture. Finally, New York University Deafness Research and Training Center is organizing a cooperative of cable television systems by which special programs for deaf viewers will become available in volume.

Manual Communication Development

The overwhelming majority of deaf people will always prefer and seek out as they always have communication that is delivered

TABLE I-IV

COLLEGE AND UNIVERSITY PROGRAMS NOW OFFERING CREDIT COURSES IN MANUAL COMMUNICATION

1. Rochester Institute of Technology, New York
2. Augustana College, Sioux Falls, South Dakota
3. Georgia State University, Atlanta
4. Northwestern University, Evanston, Illinois
5. Ohio State University, Columbus
6. University of Denver, Colorado
7. University of Akron, Ohio
8. Ohio University, Athens
9. University of Pittsburgh, Pennsylvania
10. University of Tennessee at Knoxville
11. California State University, Northridge
12. University of Northern Colorado, Greeley
13. Gallaudet College, Washington, D. C.
14. University of Illinois, Champaign
15. University of Iowa, Iowa City
16. Southern Methodist University, Dallas, Texas
17. Northern Illinois University, De Kalb
18. University of Washington, Seattle
19. Western Maryland College, Westminster
20. California State University, San Diego
21. California State University, Fresno
22. University of Wisconsin, Stevens Point
23. University of Wisconsin, Milwaukee
24. Texas Tech University, Lubbock
25. University of North Dakota, Grand Forks
26. University of Georgia, Athens
27. Florida State University, Tallahassee
28. Idaho State University, Pocatello
29. Towson State College, Maryland
30. Western Washington State College, Bellingham
31. New Mexico State University, Las Cruces
32. Texas Womans University, Denton
33. University of Southern Florida, Tampa
34. Utah State University, Logan
35. University of Utah, Salt Lake City
36. Bloomsburg State College, Pennsylvania
37. Ball State University, Muncie, Indiana
38. Oklahoma State University, Stillwater
39. Lamar University, Beaumont, Texas
40. Texas Christian University, Fort Worth
41. University of Redlands, California
42. Colorado State University, Fort Collins
43. Emory University, Atlanta, Georgia
44. Western Illinois University, Macomb
45. Purdue University, West Lafayette
46. West Virginia University, Morgantown
47. State University College of New York, Geneseo
48. Marshall University, Huntington, West Virginia

manually. The rationale is simple and obvious. It is what they understand best and easiest. It is precise, clear, easy interchange of knowledge and thinking which are basic reasons for communication. The incredible facts that sign communication has been maligned for generations and has been virtually ignored as a target for research and development despite its primary significance to almost half a million people are in themselves very revealing regarding the centuries of widespread utopianism that has provided a fertile bed for the neglect of fundamentals which have mired a substantial portion of our deaf population.

The sharp reversal of this national psychosis in recent years is borne out by the way total communication has swept the country. Further evidence lies in the scores of institutions of higher education which now give credit for sign language courses whereas five years ago only a few institutions offered such training and none gave credit (O'Rourke, 1972). Table I-IV provides a list of schools in which credit courses in sign communication have been reported.

The establishment of a system to govern the development of manual communication which presently does not have the benefit of supervision by an authoritative body is a consuming need. There is widespread interest in developing a sign language system that will approximate spoken English for classroom purposes and thus contribute to upgrading the reading and writing capabilities of deaf persons. Furthermore, the expanding use of interpreters at post-secondary and secondary programs for deaf people requires an orderly development of new sign symbols for vocabulary that is not now identified in manual communication.

The preservation and documentation of the American sign language, otherwise known as Amlesan, as a cultural heritage and for theatrical, storytelling, poetry reading purposes as well as fulfilling the in-group communication needs of the majority of deaf people is another important need.

REFERENCES

Adler, E. P. (ed.): Deafness: Research and professional training programs on deafness sponsored by the Department of Health, Education, and Welfare. *J Rehabil Deaf*, 1969, Monograph No. 1.

Craig, W. N. (ed.): Directory of Programs and Services for the Deaf in the United States. *American Ann Deaf*, 2:41-356, 1972.

Norris, A. G. (ed.): *Deafness Annual* Volume II: Contributed Papers and Reports of Research and Professional Training Programs on Deafness. Professional Rehabilitation Workers with the Adult Deaf, 1972.

O'Rourke, T. J.: National Association of the Deaf Communicative Skills Program, Progress Report No. 4. Washington, D. C. National Association of the Deaf, 1972.

Petersen, E. W. (ed.): *Deaf Leadership Training for Community Interaction.* National Association of the Deaf, Washington, D. C., 1973.

Rainer, J. D. and Altshuler, K. Z.: *Comprehensive Mental Health Services for the Deaf.* New York, Columbia University, 1966.

Rainer, J. D. and Altshuler, K. Z.: *Expanded Mental Health Care for the Deaf: Rehabilitation and Prevention.* New York, Research Foundation for Mental Hygiene, Inc., 1970.

Schein, J. D.: The National Census of the Deaf, Progress Report No. 3. Washington, National Association of the Deaf, 1971.

Schein, J. D.: *Analysis of Factors Affecting Undergraduate Enrollments at Gallaudet College.* New York, New York University, 1972.

Schlesinger, H. S. and Meadow, K. P.: *Sound and Sign.* Berkeley, University of California Press, 1972.

Stuckless, E. R. and Delgado, G. L. (eds.): *A Guide to College/Career Programs for Deaf Students.* National Technical Institute for the Deaf and Gallaudet College, 1973.

Vernon, M. and Mindel, E. G.: *They Grow in Silence.* Washington, D. C. National Association of the Deaf, 1971.

Chapter II

WORKING WITH PARENTS OF YOUNG DEAF CHILDREN

PAUL ROTTER

Prerequisites for Working With Parents
The Worker's Approach to Working With Parents
Interviewing
Meeting Parents' Needs
Preparing Parents for Peaks and Valleys
Relationship in the Home Environment
Orienting the Parent to Deafness
Conclusions

MOST PARENTS OF YOUNG DEAF children are like fish out of water. Never having had real preparation for raising any child, facing the prospect of bringing up a deaf youngster presents an overwhelmingly traumatic prospect.

In their troubled state, after discovering their child's hearing impairment, these people tend to follow a path seeking guidance and a *cure* from sympathetic friends, relatives, a variety of medical resources, social service agencies, and, in recent years, hearing and speech centers.

Ironically, the most likely center, currently available, to provide sound guidance based on years of experience in dealing with parents is often the last resource to be contacted. Thus, the family tends to reach the school for the deaf after experiencing a series of confusing and costly (emotionally as well as financially) contacts with laymen and professionals representing a broad spectrum of expertise with insignificant actual acquaintance with deafness in young deaf children.

Ideally, one qualified person should work closely with the parents to interpret past experiences, information and to coordinate future procedures. Realistically, this rarely occurs. Most parents meet many specialists on an individual basis with each one of them operating in an isolated atmosphere. Until the parent reaches a catalytic coordinator who can organize an appropriate plan of action, the parents are bound to become increasingly confused and concerned.

The bulk of this chapter will deal with the role of the person or persons who take on the responsibility for guiding the parents of young hearing impaired children. Hopefully, in the near future, professionals of ancillary disciplines will be better informed regarding the needs of these distraught parents, who actually require a variety of special services.

For the present, it is the author's premise that the guidelines to follow, supplemented by the distinctive skills of the participating specialist, will be complimentary in providing optimal assistance to the individuals so desperately in need of assistance.

Thus, this material is aimed at the teacher, clinician, therapist, pathologist, social worker, guidance counselor, houseparent, audiologist, psychologist, receptionist, physician, friend or relative interested in helping the parents at a crucial period when it is desirable to orient them to their responsibilities as well as the positive roles it is possible for them to play in raising a deaf child whose impairment is not reversible through medical treatment. Stable, knowledgeable parents are one of the child's most valuable assets and it is toward adding to *parent power* that we must direct our efforts.

PREREQUISITES FOR WORKING WITH PARENTS

When considering the needs of our prototype worker, we begin with the assumption that practicing professionals have had suitable professional preparation and have developed the necessary skills of their respective areas of specialization.

In addition, an advisor, within the context of our discussion, needs a broad source of background information regarding deafness and its limitations (real and imagined) as well as an understanding of normal child growth and development. He must also respect the functions of other professional disciplines,  that are usually effective in a multidisciplined team effort and be prepared to work with their representatives.

For his own effectiveness, it is important that he either have or makes a conscious effort to develop skill in interpreting professional knowledge into language understandable to lay parents when it relates to their current needs concerning their deaf child.

This implies that the suggestions or advice given to parents is in a form palatable to them and practical enough to be applied in their daily activities. It also assumes the counselor is secure enough to discuss all aspects of a problem and can impart information of an unpleasant or disturbing nature sensitively if it is vital at the moment. In the long run, if such details are handled skillfully, the parent will appreciate having shared such experiences in a supportive setting.

An effective parent is a powerful force toward healthy child growth and development. On the other hand, an insecure, troubled or confused parent can become a serious deterrant to normal personality development thus minimizing the possibilities for ameliorating the effects of the hearing impairment and limiting the potentials for educational progress, too.

It is, therefore, basic that we recognize how important parents are in a child's life.

In a similar vein, professionals need to begin to accept the importance of the parents as active members of the multidisciplinary team rather than exclude them as *non pros.*

It is the father or mother who is best able to provide first hand observations of the child's growth and development and his response to treatment whether it be medication, education or therapy. A most important factor in the general approach is that the parents' observations are being made in the real life setting. This is the context in which we hope our efforts will contribute toward the possibility for the youngster to make a successful adjustment.

Briefly, it is apparent that individuals working with parents of young, deaf children require specific background and training, a scientific body of knowledge, consideration for parents' needs and an ability to work on an equal partnership basis with laymen as well as professionals in the interest of providing the ultimate in service.

THE WORKER'S APPROACH TO WORKING WITH PARENTS

To establish a foundation likely to encourage rapport between a parent and a professional, real effort must be put forth to create an accepting environment.

Beginning with the physical organization of the meeting place, whether it be an office, playground or an informal setting in a corridor or lounge, extending to the worker's appearance, choice of language and general attitude, the combination has to instill in the parent a feeling of warmth, empathy and support. At the same time, the parent must gain the confidence that his counseling is coming from an objective and knowledgeable source.

An early goal for the counselor is the development of a feeling of mutual acceptance and trust in a *we centered* atmosphere. It is sometimes difficult to maintain such an ideal especially when faced with a parent who appears to be neglectful, disinterested in his child or hopelessly despondent. Frequently, such parents have understandable grounds for behaving in this manner. Within this context, it is important to remember that the hope of all parents is to have a normal healthy child, and, at one time or another, most parents do have ambivalent feelings regarding even so-called normal children.

Skilled counselors prepare themselves to anticipate a variety of possible parental attitudes from extreme negativism to the accepting, concerned parent. In spite of the broad scope, the basic approach demands a concerted effort founded on realistic optimism. Thus, once an accepting relationship has been established, the worker's immediate goal is to supplant an understandable, but unwarranted sense of pessimism, fear and guilt usually prevalent when families first became aware of their child's hearing impairment.

In a supportive milieu, it can be expected that even an unhappy parent can be encouraged to share honestly his fears, hopes, ideas and ideals.

At this point, the worker is cautioned to maintain his basic aim of working with parents rather than doing everything for them. This goal is more easily set than kept. In our frantic society, it is frequently considered easier to do things yourself in order to complete a project, but in dealing with parents, we have an obligation to guide and to help them learn the skills and attitudes needed for them to be able to raise their deaf children.

Along similar lines, it is important that we prepare ourselves to aim for attainment of reasonable goals. A counselor has to anticipate limited degrees of change, since man tends to creep rather than leap toward behavioral improvements. Developing a sense of self discipline will enable the professional to keep *hands off* and will go far towards shielding him from actually doing too much for parents, who in their anguish and uncertainty tend to lean too heavily towards allowing an unsophisticated worker to assume parental obligations.

Expecting too rapid a change, too great an improvement in parent behavior or moving toward a professionally oriented goal rather than working toward a parent centered cooperatively sought end frequently proves frustrating and disappointing to both participants, the parent as well as the counselor. The result is often a feeling of failure that is only too obvious to an already upset father or mother.

Such disturbing occurrences can be avoided through foresight and sensitive anticipation in preparation for dealing with specific problem areas.

Confidentiality

Another area for professional concern is the need to respect the privacy of the home. This aspect of the parent-counselor relationship is often overlooked even by experienced workers. As a result, it is much too common an occurrence in which parents' most sensitive and private thoughts are discussed among staff members in semi-public settings. Professionals should exercise extreme caution. First, to be certain that only when essential will confidential information be shared with other staff members and secondly, that all such discussions be held in areas that will insure the maintenance of the parent's faith in his counselor.

Once the parent's belief in his advisor is shaken, the professional has seriously limited his value to the parent group as a whole, the children and other professional people faced with the task of helping the family.

Flexibility

In order to create a working relationship with a parent, at the onset we must start with the premise that the parents, child or family is unique. They are likely to be different from the case or client you handled earlier in the day or yesterday or the week or month before.

It is, therefore, important that the worker equip himself for these differences with a variety of techniques and a willingness to adapt his approach towards meeting the requirements of the immediate situation.

This calls for an ability to respond readily to changes of mood; to react successfully to all levels of understanding and to expect differing degrees of ability or willingness to cooperate on the part of the parents.

To cope favorably with so many dynamic factors, professional responsibility demands continuous efforts to improve one's skill and to acquire and practice new approaches through further education, participation in seminars and keeping abreast of the most recent research in the major field of interest as well as in ancillary areas.

However, most important of all is a practical application of an individualized approach in working with parents.

An initial step in this direction is delving deeply enough into the situation to be able to discover the real needs of the person facing you. For some people, the need may merely be for accurate information, for others emotional support and for still others the need may be for assistance beyond the limits of the worker's own capabilities. In the latter case, the professional is actually being most helpful in honestly acknowledging his limitations and then referring the parent to the proper resource.

Evaluation

At this point, it is pertinent to remind the reader that he must recognize the difficulty he faces in evaluating his own *modus operandi.*

As in all behavioral approaches, objective standards and measuring techniques are only now being developed. Standardized, objective testing procedures are not presently available for application to counseling.

If the parent appears to relate well, communicates meaningfully, seems willing to continue to come for assistance and is able to obtain satisfactory solutions to current difficulties, the counselor has good reason to believe he is operating adequately.

INTERVIEWING

Although numerous books and articles have been devoted to interviewing techniques, limited consideration to this area is warranted at this time due to the critical importance interviewing plays in the parent-worker relationship.

It is worth noting that all of the previously discussed attitudes of the professional are directly related to the interview exchange.

No matter which specialist assumes the role of parental advisor, he does so by means of communicating with the specific father or mother. Most interchanges are direct and verbal, but they may also include written or manual forms, the use of a third party interpreter or some combination of these in order to give and/or get information.

Whichever means of communicating is used, the interviewer has to be certain to interpret the parents' responses objectively without allowing personal opinions or biases to distort his concepts. The accuracy of the advisor's interpretations are a crucial factor contributing toward the possibility of providing effective guidance.

With a basic desire to help people plus an amalgamation of training and experience, it is necessary to develop the ability to listen with a third ear and to learn to really comprehend the underlying meaning of the parents' responses; the content frequently differs considerably from the literal interpretation.

It is important either early in the interview or prior to its beginning that both participants understand clearly why they are meeting and what they hope to achieve as a result of their efforts. In far too many instances, the interview tends to become a rambling discussion only because clear-cut goals are not well defined at the onset.

From the interviewer's position, an attempt is being made to acquire necessary background information related to the parents' problem and verify the facts. Then, in the light of this information, unique professional skills are employed to assist the parent in alleviating his immediate difficulty.

Unless specific details are required, the most productive questioning employs the form of open ended queries. For example, asking, "Does your child wear his hearing aid?" usually will result in a *yes* or *no* answer. However, asking, "How does Billy respond to wearing his aid?" will usually result in answers relating to frequency of usage, response to sound, voice changes and so forth.

Care should be taken in posing questions in order that the interviewer avoid forcing an answer he would like to receive or one that the respondent feels the interviewer would like to have. Relating, once again, to hearing aids, in a school or clinic where their usage is urged, an interviewer who asks, "He does wear his hearing aid most of the time, doesn't he?" is more than likely to get a positive though not necessarily accurate answer.

Another element related to making optional use of questions is the timing aspect. Sitting through periods of silence can prove disturbing even to experienced interviewers, but such pauses are effective means for allowing or forcing the parent to clarify or qualify a previous statement. In many instances, it is helpful to encourage a speaker with slight leads such as, "Go on," "What does that mean?," "How does that affect him?"

On the other hand, some parents really need time to gather their thoughts before elaborating. Experience usually aids the interviewer in his decision as to whether he should pose a leading question or simply stand by awaiting additional information.

This much too brief presentation of the interview process merely touches on a few of the fundamental details. Acquiring skill in interviewing is best done through practice under skilled supervision. Such practice can be supplemented by taping interviews and then studying them critically with the assistance of a more experienced interviewer.

For those interested in studying interview techniques, a series of taped interviews have become available recently and may be purchased through Year Book Medical Publishers, Inc., 35 East Wacker Drive, Chicago, Illinois 60601.

It appears fairly obvious that if the practitioner is to give parents the full benefit of his particular specialty, he must certainly acquire a suitable technique for communicating effectively in a face to face relationship.

MEETING PARENTS' NEEDS

At an early point in the deaf child's life, his parents are in desperate need of locating the ear of a professional whose manner indicates a sincere desire to listen, explain, support and encourage a future plan of action.

Essential in fulfilling this need for the parents is recognition of the anguish and indecision they face as individuals as well as the complexities of their role in the family and in the community. It takes a great deal of courage on the part of the mother and father who have to accept the role of raising a disabled youngster while fulfilling all the other demands of family life in today's complex society. To instill this confidence and courage, a counselor must be able to put himself in the parent's position. He may then be able to develop the insight necessary to enable him to establish a relationship in which he will be *heard* and his guidance accepted.

Sensitivity concerning cultural roles and the stresses of modern urban society must also be developed. One has to recognize how differently families representing a variety of socioeconomic backgrounds consider physical impairment or the responsibility of raising a child who is *different*.

Some parents hope, others pray that the hearing impairment will be only a temporary affliction and things will soon return to normal. Other parents rush with the youngster from one specialist to another and then on to unscrupulous miracle workers in search of a nonexistent cure at costs far beyond their financial means. Still others, even in our times, hide either their disabled child or themselves, regarding the child's impairment as something shameful or hopeless.

Fortunately, most parents, in spite of their negative feelings, are determined to find out what can be done rationally and to do what is best for their child.

The individual serving as the family counselor must set a priority on working with the individuals within the family constellation to orient and unite them in a direct effort for the good of the child.

With these factors in mind, the worker begins by accepting people as they are and he then encourages movement toward mutually acceptable goals aimed at helping the individuals function more effectively as parents of a disabled child. This is a critical element contributing to the possibility of a successful endeavor, since current research indicates that parents' acceptance of conditions or acceptance of objective evidence is an essential in having them take an accepting attitude to their deaf child and his future needs.

Along similar lines, it has been shown in educational as well as therapeutic work that intrinsic motivation to learn or to come and be helped is another essential element contributing towards success as contrasted to the use of the threat of failure (either the parents' or the child's) or the process of aiming for artificial goals set by the professional. Stated simply, the parents benefit the most, when they come for help willingly rather than appear as a result of pressure by an agency or individual implying that as parents they should feel obligated to do so.

For success, the professional needs to inspire or convince the parents that he is capable of providing the *something* that is needed at various stages in order to help them do what is best for their child.

PREPARING PARENTS FOR PEAKS AND VALLEYS

During the various stages of a child's development, there will be highs and lows. Concerned parents' feelings may be expected to fluctuate accordingly. The counselor has to anticipate such occurrences. He, therefore, prepares parents for such eventualities, tempers overoptimism and makes himself available for support when things do not appear too well in the parents' eyes. These are, indeed, the times that try the souls of the professional as well as the parents.

It is relatively easy to share the pleasures of parents who hear the first intelligible word from their deaf child or see the child's first accurate responses to amplified sound. To a sensitive counselor, it is a mutually moving experience to hear a troubled parent state that their in-laws, their own parents or anyone else believes he or she is directly responsible for their baby's hearing disability, an inability to speak, or attain toilet training as rapidly as they would have these milestones reached. These are the opportune times for the effective counselor to really do his thing to help the discouraged parent pick himself up to move through the crisis toward further progress.

In truth, we need each other (parents and professionals) and the child needs us. It is more than mere words and must take shape in a plan of action directed by the counselor once this opportunity is presented.

RELATIONSHIPS IN THE HOME ENVIRONMENT

In addition to some of the previously described crises which the worker must be prepared to help mothers and fathers face, he may have to act as the coagulant for a shaky marital relationship. Although the conditions for breaking up a marriage may have existed for some time, the arrival of a deaf child can prove to be the catalyst unless the counselor can be effective in either resolving the problem or guiding the parents to an appropriate resource for necessary long term therapy.

Parents will require support in recognizing that hearing siblings in a family may be expected from time to time to use the hearing impaired child as an outlet for their own emotional needs.

Grandparents, friends, relatives, neighbors and strangers in the community can be unconsciously cruel to an overly sensitive parent subjected to well meaning but disparaging remarks regarding the deaf youngster. As a result, supportive counseling may be required to assure the troubled parent that there really is no operation to cure the child's deafness; a school for the deaf is the currently valid placement for a specific child; the child really needs a costly hearing aid and can benefit from auditory training even though he is profoundly deaf. These are but a few of the more positive aspects to be developed in response to the multitude of embarrassing and troublesome statements or questions most parents of deaf children hear at one time or another.

ORIENTING THE PARENT TO DEAFNESS

If parents are fortunate, they come into contact with a skilled, knowledgeable counselor early in their travels. It is, however, more likely that even though they may have been in contact with a number of agencies or disciplines, they remain rather naive regarding the implications of hearing impairments for the growth and development of a deaf child. In addition, although parents use the terminology of the field freely, careful discussion usually reveals them to have either a limited or distorted understanding of the professional jargon.

The implications are fairly obvious. Careful counseling calls for explanations regarding the physical limitations of the child's hearing threshold, the potential values of amplification, special education programs, the various means of communicating with deaf people from purely oral through purely manual approaches, recognized medical facilities, toilet training, setting limits and all other phases of life experience.

Along with this broad overview, it is important to explain to parents in language they can understand, current research findings that are applicable to their own current questions.

Cumulative experience in dealing with parents has shown that labels placed on children and professional terminology that is misinterpreted are not only misleading, but actually frightening to the parent who has had little or no previous contact with profound deafness. Careful, understandable explanations, by the worker for the parent, of the basic vocabulary of the field will do much to relieve tensions while helping the family understand the status and needs of the young child.

Such terms as communication skills, speech, language, lip (speech) reading, oral-aural, manual, sign language, total communication, cued speech, audiogram, hearing (loss) threshold, audiometer, decibels, deaf, hard of hearing, mild-severe and profound hearing losses are examples of commonly used terms and needs to be clearly understood by the parents as they come into contact with them.

The professional counselor also has an ethical responsibility for providing each parent with an objective review of the types of educational settings available to deaf children internationally as contrasted to what may be available to the child on a local level. Then descriptions should include resident, day programs, integrated opportunities (with a number of variations), resource rooms, tutorial programs, part time hearing school, school for deaf placement or any combination of these programs.

Even though adulthood may appear to be unthinkably far ahead, this is an opportune time to discuss long term future goals while introducing parents to descriptions of capable deaf adults participating in all sorts of daily life activities.

Where possible, parents should be provided with opportunities to meet and to socialize with successful deaf adults, who can usually be located in almost any urban center or through the alumni associations of the established schools for the deaf.

CONCLUSION

It is probably obvious that this chapter contains little or no reference to an organized program for working with parent groups nor was there time spent on describing the professional as a group leader. The omission is deliberate, since both aspects are included in a detailed description of a parents program in a school for the deaf (Rotter, 1969) and is available in a previously published manuscript.

The current emphasis has been an attempt to provide practical assistance for professional personnel representing a variety of disciplines concerned with helping mothers and fathers to cope successfully with the problems they encounter in raising a hearing impaired child.

When successful, they make it possible for the families to face reality, set up reasonable routines, set realistic goals and work cooperatively with individuals as well as agencies whose major aim is to help the deaf child make his way toward a wholesome adult life.

REFERENCES

Rotter, P.: Human relations in parent education, *The Volta Rev,* 59 (1): 20-24, January, 1957.

Rotter, P.: A guide for educating parents of deaf children. *The Volta Rev,* *60* (1):28-32, January, 1958.

Rotter, P.: The relationship between the educator and parents of deaf children. *The Volta Rev,* *60* (7):370-371, September, 1958.

Rotter, P.: The parents association in the school for the deaf. *The Volta Rev,* *65* (6):296-298, June, 1963.

Rotter, P.: *A Parents Program in a School for the Deaf,* Washington, D. C.: Alexander G. Bell Association for the Deaf, Inc., 114 pp., 1969.

Chapter III

THE EARLY DETECTION OF HEARING LOSS

John A. Grant

1. What does early detection really mean?
2. Does the concept of early detection have particular application to the condition of hearing loss?
3. What are the common causes and treatments of hearing loss?
4. What are the available screening techniques for the early detection of hearing loss?
5. What are the essential elements of a good hearing screening program?
6. What benefits may be expected from such a program?
7. What are some of the pitfalls and problems to watch for and avoid?

THE EARLY DETECTION PROCESS

An ounce of prevention is worth a pound of cure. Who hasn't heard that old chestnut? It is still true today and in fact is the basis for one of the dominant philosophies of public health.

The objective of the early detection process is to find people who have diseases they do not know they have and get them under treatment before progression to disability or death takes place. Early detection can be practiced through a variety of techniques including personal suspicion of illness, routine physical examination, and mass technical screening. Of these, mass screening has been proven over the years to be the most effective and efficient method of disease control in a defined population.

The early detection of inapparent illness is in reality a sophisticated form of disease prevention. Any well defined group of people may be expected to have, upon proper examination, predictable numbers of certain diseases. Many of these people will be unaware or only vaguely aware that they have some progressive illness. It is at this point that timely intervention can be highly effective. Diseases caught in early stages are easier to cure, and the curative process is usually less costly to everyone.

The most simple form of early disease detection is reporting to your family doctor when you have some vague feeling of illness. Your complaint may range from *just not feeling right* to a definite pain or physical change somewhere in your body. After a few careful questions, a physical examination, and perhaps some laboratory studies your physician may be able to make a firm diagnosis and hopefully prescribe a successful treatment. For decades, authorities in the health sciences have encouraged people to get routine physical examinations. This suggestion has been based on the belief that physical examination will detect most incipient illness even before the prospective patient feels that vague impulse to visit his physician. However, this practice has been proven to be rather costly and relatively ineffective.[1] It has been largely abandoned in recent years in favor of the process of mass technical screening: the primary subject of this chapter.

Health screening is a technical procedure that divides an apparently well population into two groups—those with a high probability of a particular disease and those with a low prob-

1. A. Yankauer and R. A. Lawrence: "A study of periodic school medical examinations." *American Journal of Public Health* 45:71 (1955).

ability of that same disease.[2] In the process of screening, a diagnosis is not made by professional workers. Rather, those persons who *fail* the screening test are referred on to a diagnostic and treatment facility where they are then considered to have a specific probability of having a particular disease. On the positive side, those persons who *pass* the screening test have an equally specific probability of health, defined as the absence of disease.[3] Thus, mass technical screening becomes a powerful administrative tool for the direction of patients to the proper health care facility at the proper time.

APPLICATION TO HEARING LOSS

Hutchinson, writing in 1960, was one of the first authors to explore the logic of the suitability of any particular disease to the screening process.[4] He pointed out that a *good screening disease* is one that exists before a person is aware of it, can be detected by simple clinical techniques, can be cured, and is sufficiently common to justify an organized program effort.

Diseases suitable to the screening process must have a fairly long period of incubation before they surface and make the patient sick. It would, for example, be futile to screen for an acute and rapidly progressive disease like spinal meningitis. In this disease, the patient becomes ill rapidly with a dramatic and typical set of symptoms and progresses on to a stage of death or disability if appropriate treatment is not instituted on an emergency basis. On the other hand, a condition like cancer of the cervix may be present in an unsuspecting woman for years before symptoms of pain and bleeding call attention to its presence. In the latter case, a simple PAP smear or clinical examination may have revealed the condition in early stages and led to the institution of a lifesaving operative procedure.

---

2. J. A. Grant: "The administrator looks at mass screening." *Perspectives in Maternal and Child Health,* School of Hygiene and Public Health, The Johns Hopkins University, Series B, No. 2 (November 1970).

3. H. Anderson: "Screening to Detect Health." *New England Journal of Medicine* 283:492 (1970).

4. G. B. Hutchinson: "Evaluation of Preventive Services." *Journal of Chronic Diseases* 11:497-508 (1960).

The ideal screening procedure employs a simple technical device which may be operated with ease and repetition. In this way, nonprofessional personnel with minimal training can process large numbers of candidates in a short period of time. The electrocardiograph would be an example of a poor screening device. The tracing is obtained with difficulty by a highly trained technician and must be interpreted by a qualified and experienced physician. Furthermore, it produces a relatively useless bit of information if not accompanied by a great deal of supportive clinical data. In contrast, a simple Snellen *E* chart costs only a few dollars, can be used by virtually anyone with a few hours of training, and has extremely specific cutoff points for referral leading to the frequent detection of serious and potentially blinding disorders of the eye.[5]

A disease must exist in sufficient prevalence in a population to be worth an administrator's time and effort. The phonocardioscan, an ingenius electronic device which detects serious heart murmurs in children, has virtually passed out of use because the problems it can detect have proven to be so rare. By the time the child is old enough to tolerate the test, his murmur has usually been detected by some other means or it is indicative of a cardiac condition not amenable to existing methods of therapy. Nevertheless, the device retains some popularity because it is so attractive and easy to use. In a similar way, mass screening for phenylketonuria (PKU) looked so promising a decade ago that many states passed laws requiring all newborn infants to be screened for the disease. It was argued that the disease, when caught early, could be treated effectively by diet and that many cases of mental retardation would actually be prevented. Who could argue against that? As it turns out, the disease is extremely rare (less than one case in every 100,000 newborn infants), exists in some forms harmless to the individual, and is extremely difficult to treat. The rigid diet necessary for the control of the condition has been found frequently to produce serious consequences of its own. As a result, the scientific and legal basis of

5. A. Patz and R. Hoover: "Protection of vision in children" (Springfield, Charles C Thomas, Publisher, 1969).

this mass detection effort has been seriously questioned. At the other extreme, a disease like dental decay is too common to warrant mass screening. Recent surveys of inner-city children by dental scientists from the University of Maryland have shown that 73 percent of prekindergarten children have serious problems requiring immediate treatment. Why screen for something almost everybody has? There isn't even enough money to take care of the dental decay people complain about everyday.

The condition of hearing loss fits all of Hutchinson's criteria for detection by mass technical screening. A deaf infant doesn't know he can't hear and may experience grave developmental problems because of inability to relate to his peer group. Acid rock music fans and boiler factory workers may find suddenly after many years of auditory abuse that people are having to shout at them to get their attention. And hearing loss is common. At least five percent of school age children[6] and even more adults have a significant degree of hearing loss needing professional attention. Fortunately, most forms of the disease can be detected easily and treated successfully.

CAUSES AND TREATMENTS

The human organism is in danger of the acquisition of hearing loss from infancy to old age. The major causes of hearing loss are congenital nerve deficiency, repetitive or chronic middle ear infection, nerve damage from excessive auditory fatigue, advanced age, and space occupying lesions, such as acoustic neuroma. Some of the causes of hearing loss are preventable, some are curable, but most can be ameliorated in some fashion or another.

Babies born with hearing loss due to a defective acoustic nerve, are rare, except during epidemics of congenital rubella (German measles).[7] Extensive screening of infants in newborn

6. United States Department of Health, Education, and Welfare, Public Health Service, National Institute of Health, National Institute of Neurological Disease and Blindness. Human Communication: "The Public Health Aspects of Hearing, Language and Speech Disorders" (Washington, D. C., Government Printing Office, 1968) (PHS Publication No. 1754), p. 3.

7. J. Hardy: "Rubella and its aftermath." *Children* 16:91-96 (1969).

nurseries has been disappointing and is probably wasteful of valuable professional time. However, it must be remembered that the rewards are great when remediation of congenitally deaf children is begun at the earliest possible age. Middle ear infection (otitis media) is the great silent crippler of the middle ear. Ear infections are extremely common in children and occur with great frequency during the preschool and early school years. Many children in this age group do not know they have ear infections and do not complain about them. For example, fourteen percent of children waiting for nonmedical services in a large pediatric clinic in Baltimore were found to have some form of middle ear infection.[8] Nerve damage due to excessive noise levels has become all too common in modern society. Loud music, lawn mowers, and sporting weapons, all take their daily toll. As people live longer, their chance of becoming deaf from simple aging increases. Deafness from tumors and other lesions pressing on the acoustic nerve are rare although symptomatically characteristic.

Mass immunization against rubella is expected to virtually eliminate nerve deafness from this tragic disease. On the other hand, a staggering amount of hearing loss could be prevented by the early, vigorous, and complete treatment of middle ear infection with antibiotic drugs and the avoidance of or protection from excessive noise levels. The high prevalence of middle ear infection clearly indicates mass otoscopic screening of preschool and school age children wherever they congregate. While most of the common antibiotics are effective against middle ear infection, physicians commonly fail to prescribe the medication for sufficient lengths of time and parents commonly fail to give it everyday as prescribed. Protective ear devices in noisy industrial settings and during the pursuit of hobbies such as claybird shooting are increasing in popularity, although leave much to be desired in terms of comfort and proven effectiveness. Many individuals are content to accept the penalty of some degree of hearing loss in the pursuit of their work or pleasure. Finally, and unfortunately, there is no cure, as yet, for old age.

---

8. J. A. Grant, R. Hepner and E. L. Morton: "Evaluating performance of the physician's assistant." *Clinical Pediatrics* 11:685-686 (1972).

When prevention fails, remediation takes over. Techniques in education for the deaf are elegant and widely available. When sound levels cannot be boosted through the use of hearing aids and other devices, techniques such as lipreading and sign language often prove to be gratifying aids to communication.

SCREENING TECHNIQUES

A variety of techniques for the detection of hearing loss are available. Among the more successful have been the Ewing test, puretone audiometry, communication checklists, and developmental landmark scales. Each screening device or technique carries with it precision and reliability factors of mathematical predictability. Measurement of these qualities can be used not only in the selection of instruments but also for program evaluation.

The Ewing test for early preschool children simply involves the physical response of a child turning his head in the direction of an attractive noise. Good data on the precision and reliability of this interesting test are not available. Auditory acuity can be tested with greater confidence in late preschool age by means of puretone audiometry. Would-be screeners are well advised to avoid simple instruments producing only a few tones and to seek standard screening audiometers capable of both sweepcheck and threshold testing. Checklists that monitor the growth of communicative skills and developmental sampling devices such as the Denver Developmental Screening Test have experienced increasing use in recent years.[9] They may be strong indicators of hearing impairment by measuring the consequences of hearing rather than the ability to hear itself.

Any screening device can and should be subjected to rigorous tests of its precision and reliability prior to actual program use. In order to do this, it is necessary to compare the performance of the screening device to some diagnostic standard. For example, the results of screening audiometry should be compared to audiometric testing by a competent professional audiometrist. The degree to which the screening device can predict hearing

---

9. W. F. Frankenburg and J. B. Dodds: "The Denver Development Screening Test." *Journal of Pediatrics* 71:181 (1967).

loss or normal hearing is a measure of its value in the process of early detection. Some common measures of the value of a screening instrument are sensitivity, specificity, and the use of a correlation coefficient.[10] Sensitivity is the probability that a given test will correctly identify a diseased person. Specificity is the probability that a given test will correctly identify a non-diseased person. A correlation coefficient is a composite rating of both sensitivity and specificity on a numerical scale ranging from 0 (no correlation) to 1.0 (perfect correlation). By the use of such measures, a screening test can be related to the ideal or can be compared with another screening test.

Once the inherent qualities of a given screening device are known, these same mathematical measures can be used to evaluate programs in which the device is employed. Simple administrative record keeping of the screening process and periodic feedback from the diagnostic and treatment source allow the administrator to compare the performance of the screening device at any given time to a previously set standard. In this way, whole populations may be assured of either disease or health, caseloads arriving at the diagnostic and treatment centers may be predicted, and close cost accounting for disease control can be tallied.[2] There is urgent need to employ sound quantitative management techniques in the field of health services, particularly where early detection is an important activity.

HEARING SCREENING PROGRAMS

A judicious amount of planning is vital to program success. Successful administrators take care to avoid the extremes of anti-planning and over-planning. In any good basic plan, the administrator will carefully identify his goals to be reached, the activities by means of which he hopes to reach them, and the resources at his command for program operation.[11] Careful rec-

10. J. A. Grant and A. M. Gittelsohn: "The Denver Developmental Screening Test compared with the Stanford-Binet Test. Evaluation of 298 preschool children." *Health Services Reports* 87:473-476 (1972).

11. O. L. Denniston, I. M. Rosenstock and V. A. Getting: "Evaluation of program effectiveness." *Public Health Reports* 83:323-335 (1968).

ords should be kept during the various program stages—planning, implementation, and evaluation.[12]

Ask any of your friends to tell you about the game of baseball. He will invariably enter upon a discourse of pitching, catching, batting, and base running. He will probably neglect, in his fervor, to tell you that the object of the game is to get the runners over home plate. He will forget to tell you what they expect to achieve. In response to a question about goals, you may hear something like, "We intend to do hearing screening on every child in Central City." Screening is just one program activity. The real or ultimate goal is to cure every case of hearing loss in Central City. And this implies that a whole series of subgoals or program goals must be reached along the way, the activities of referral, follow-up, diagnosis, and treatment moving the child from stage to stage.

In program planning, novice administrators generally start with an activity they intend to perform and then fit goals, resources and everything else around it. This is the tail wagging the dog to be sure. The only consideration of activities should be activity *selection*. What are the alternate activities by which a specified goal could be reached? What are the relative costs of these various activities? Is somebody already doing it? Has it already been done? These can prove to be very embarrassing questions to impatient people who are more intent on *doing their thing* than they are on getting the thing done.

Resource availability is inevitably a restrictive force on programming. It may dictate the amount of goal that can be reached. It may dictate the kind of activity to be employed. It may dictate that there will be no program at all at some point in time. It has been this author's experience that resource availability is usually the starting point in health programming, rather than merely the price tag placed on a program designed to reach a desirable set of goals. The usual sequence is that a sum of

---

12. J. J. Dempsey and J. A. Grant: "Viewing program evaluation as a component of the administrative process: The RAGPIE Model, *Perspectives in Maternal and Child Health,* School of Hygiene and Public Health, The Johns Hopkins University, Series B, No. 4 (September 1971).

money becomes available through some agency for a vaguely specified set of program activities, and the hapless administrator is forced into a struggle to find a set of goals acceptable to the funder. How much better off we would all be if the sequence were reversed.

One last word of caution on program management: Grant's Law. There are three essential conditions which must be satisfied before a program can be completed successfully. First, there must be demonstrated need for the program. Second, the administrator of the program must have the legal authority to conduct the program. Third, and most important, money must be available to carry the program to reasonable conclusion. If any one of these three elements is missing, the effort is almost certainly doomed to failure.

BENEFITS

What can one expect from a good hearing screening program?

The early identification of hearing loss at almost any age but especially in infancy and childhood, is a gift of untold value. The process of learning, nature's most precious gift, takes place in large part through auditory pathways. A child who never hears learns to live in a distorted and unreal world. The hell of deafness in later years can be squelched by protection from noise in youth and the prompt and thorough treatment of infection. The earlier the treatment, the lower the cost, and the better the results. If one's goal is truly to eliminate the disease of hearing loss in a specific population, early detection and prompt treatment through mass screening affords the most effective and efficient method of disease control. Disease control through screening is not cheaper than treatment of episodic disease; it is better, and it is the only proven method of getting the job done in a complete and thorough way.

PITFALLS AND PROBLEMS

The author has worked in both administrative and research capacities in a number of screening programs and has observed errors in judgment and execution which seem to recur with regularity. A brief catalogue of some of the more common screening program pitfalls is offered in the spirit of helping those considering the use of screening methodology to avoid the obvious. Some careful scientists and skilled administrators have admitted their mistakes so that we all can learn.

A. *Screening as a program entity.* In our experience, the most common pitfall is to perceive a screening activity as being complete in itself rather than merely a part of an overall health services program. The process of screening is exciting to plan and seems enormously productive. However, administrators frequently forget the follow-up phase of screening and can never then collect the important evaluation data they need. When confronted with this observation the administrator often replies, "Well, at least we are pointing up needs." But even this may not be true. As we have seen, screening can only ever classify a population into probability groups (hence the danger of *population description* through screening). In the context of a complete health services program, classification of the service populations by screening is only a sub-objective to the ultimate objective of disease control.

B. *Economy through screening.* Screening is often justified on the basis of immediate dollar savings to the service delivery system. Careful cost accounting, which is almost never done, will show that this is almost never true. It stands to reason that the more disease one looks for, the more disease one finds. Screening may be a more efficient way to eradicate some disease, but it will certainly increase overall program costs directed toward that disease. It is often cited that technical personnel or even volunteers can be used in screening, thereby cutting costs. While it is true that technicians cost less than doctors or nurses, one would probably not have employed high priced professionals to do screening in the first place. A screening program usually represents an absolute, new expenditure in an aggressive approach to disease control which will also increase the need for additional follow-up by professional personnel. However, this should not be a deterrent to screening; look at what you have done in addition to how much money you have spent.

C. *There ought to be a law.* Screening is a pet activity of the health legislator. Public health workers (and, unfortunately, inventors of screening devices) have, on occasion, invited such legislation. It sounds like a reasonable activity, for example, to require tuberculosis testing of all school children. The legislator envisions the eradication of a dread disease by a stroke of the governor's pen. Once a program idea with this kind of appeal catches fire, no one may bother to ask critical planning questions such as prevalance of reactors in the projected population, extent of coverage of existing programs, location of particularly high risk groups, or the priority that should be assigned to screening school children in an overall tuberculosis program; categorical resources might be better spent on the more adequate treatment of known active cases and reactors.

D. *The only alternative.* Screening has been a favored activity of health departments, volunteer groups, departments of education and professions whose activities are restricted by law because it is frequently their only possible or permissible kind of activity. Health departments have traditionally avoided therapeutic activity, in deference to the practitioner, except with the most destitute populations. Volunteer organizations tend to be organ-oriented or disease-oriented (eye, ear, heart, diabetes, etc.) and of course cannot render treatment; they are fond of *pointing up needs,* usually under the label of *health education.* Educators are justly concerned about the *organs of learning* and frequently anxious about completeness of coverage among their charges, direction of education services to a defined population (as best they can) is mandated by law and is one of their strong points, frequently spilling over into the health field. Dental physicians have proposed culturing the tonsils for streptococcus (one inch away!) and optometrists, limited to refraction and exercise, can hardly be blamed for vigorous activity in screening for ocular disease. A persistent, resourceful administrator will invariably work around his constraints and adopt program activities which are at least legal, if not useful.

E. *Technological seduction.* We have seen many instances of irrational planning due to infatuation with gadgetry rather than program purpose. The salesman offering a complicated optical device (circa $300.00) can produce an endless list of reasons why his machine is superior to a simple Snellen Chart (circa $3.00), most of them either unfounded or insignificant. Thoughtful administrators have run aground on the rocks of computerization. Computers only facilitate the speed of data processing and can never correct fuzzy thinking. Trailer fetish (unnatural love of mobile units) has led to many an uncalibrated machine, a blown fuse, a cold, wet, uncomfortable clientele, and an empty pocketbook. The most elegant, efficient, and effective screening machine with dials, knobs, and flashing lights may be useful only for a disease that is so rare that cost-benefit becomes ludicrous, placing the administrator in the unenviable position of trying to defend, rather than evaluate, his program.

Once specific program goals have been delineated, the administrator chooses from a wide variety of possible program activities those which are available, appropriate, efficient, effective, and economical. In pursuit of the eradication of hearing loss from a defined population, mass technical screening may well be the best alternative.

CONCLUSION

What does early detection really mean? Early detection of a disease is the process of discovering it before irrevocable disability or death occurs. Early detection is best carried out before the patient actually has symptoms. The most effective and efficient method of early disease detection is mass technical screening.

Does the concept of early detection have particular application to the condition of hearing loss? Yes. Hearing loss is a condition of high prevalence. It is frequently caused by disease that can either be cured or at least greatly relieved. It exists in an inapparent or subclinical stage in many forms from birth to old age. It can be detected by simple mechanical techniques by persons with minimal training.

What are the common causes and treatments of hearing loss? Congenital nerve damage, middle ear infection, nerve damage from noise, aging, and space taking lesions pressing the acoustic nerve are the most common causes of hearing loss. The prevention of maternal rubella through immunization, the prompt and thorough treatment of middle ear disease with antibiotics, and protection from excessive noise levels are highly effective in reducing the prevalence of hearing loss.

What are the available screening techniques for the early detection of hearing loss? The Ewing directional test, puretone audiometry, communication checklists, and developmental landmark scales have all been used for the early detection of hearing loss. The most effective and efficient method from late preschool age to old age is puretone audiometry.

What are the essential elements of a good hearing screening program? Careful assessment of goals to be reached, activities to be employed, and resources to support them are essential concepts for the program planner. A thoughtful plan, supportive implementation, and realistic evaluation are essential in good program management. In every successful program, there is demonstrated need for the service, clear authority for management, and realistic funding to see the program through.

What benefits may be expected from such a program? Hearing is essential to the communicative process which is, in turn, essential to normal development and a high quality of life. Disease control through mass screening, if properly conducted, is the most effective and efficient means of eliminating hearing loss in a defined population.

What are some of the pitfalls and problems to watch for and avoid? Considering screening as an end in itself, hoping for super-economical program operation, evoking legal mandate, failing to examine all possible program alternatives, and falling victim to technological seduction are common failings of the screening program administrator. Nevertheless, screening remains a powerful program alternative if it is placed in the context of contributing to the ultimate goal of disease eradication.

Chapter IV

THE TOTALLY DEAF, THE DEAFENED, THE HARD OF HEARING AND THE HARD OF HEARING SIGNER

S. JAMES CUTLER

THE PROBLEM OF REHABILITATING the hearing impaired in recent years has taken on new impetus with expansion of overall services to this group of handicapped persons. Across the nation and abroad large groups of organizations are decrying the fact that the numbers of hearing disability individuals rehabilitated are small. Stress is now being placed by national organizations for the deaf, to encourage states to hire coordinators and specialists who have been trained in communication methods to set up specific programs for this type of disabled individual. Unfortunately, in this writer's opinion, the emphasis will be directed toward the totally deaf group that has been residentially trained in manualism and signs; while the so-called orally trained deaf and the hard of hearing and speech handicapped will receive little, if any, added attention. Perhaps new organizations oriented to the latter group are indicated to promote pressure for more action for these disabled individuals. Along with the above comments will be the everlasting reaction that individuals with hearing and speech problems decry being classified as disabled, handicapped, etc.

One of the weaknesses seen in today's training programs for rehabilitation personnel is the lack of understanding of the terminology of the different categories of the hearing impaired. Unless one has been indoctrinated by actual specifics with illustrations and examples, it is difficult to conceive that there are actual differences among the so-called totally deaf. There are significant differences between the so-called hard of hearing and those individuals who are classified as hard of hearing signers. For those who desire to develop this understanding and accept and realize these differences in classification, this chapter is being written.

The Conference of Executives American Schools for the Deaf came out with an excellent set of definitions a few years back (1937) to once and for all classify: *The Deaf* and the *Hard of Hearing* (Davis and Silverman, 1960). Although specific and to the point in classification, there are additional factors to be considered which will define more clearly to rehabilitation counselors and coordinators and also other interested individuals what really constitutes the individual with his specific type of communication problem. With this in mind, this writer, as a professor of aural rehabilitation and lecturer in audiology, developed the following terminology to present to his graduate students:

1. Totally deaf, unable to speak: An individual with no residual hearing, inability to talk, educated in a residential school for the deaf, means of communication are through manual alphabet and sign language or pencil and paper.
2. Totally deaf, with deaf speech, but refuses to speak: An individual with no residual hearing, can speak (quality poor), educated in a residential school for the deaf, means of communication are through manual alphabet and sign language or pencil and paper.
3. Totally deaf, oralist: An individual with no residual hearing but wears hearing aid in many cases to keep him aware of sounds in his environment, has excellent deaf speech, educated in an oral oriented residential school for day classes for the deaf, means of communication strictly through reading lips. Many of these individuals resent being handed a pencil and pad or being asked to read a written message.
4. Deafened: An individual who has had normal hearing and speech but is now totally deaf. He or she has been educated in regular schools for normal hearing. Their means of communication now are by reading the lips of whoever is speaking to them or by pencil and pad. Their speech gradually deteriorates over a period of time but is quite understandable.
5. Hard of Hearing: An individual who has a partial loss of hearing

function, may be aided by medical or surgical treatment or amplification electronically or vocally. He has been educated in regular schools for normal hearing. His means of communication is by having speech sounds amplified and his speech is affected by the degree of loss of hearing.

6. Hard of Hearing Signer: An individual who has a partial loss of hearing, usually refuses amplification. He or she failed in regular public school and thus was educated in a residential school for the deaf where he learned to communicate through use of the manual alphabet and sign language. Sometimes he is referred to as being *communicatively lazy.* He can hear with amplification and he can speak but prefers to use the language of signs and finger spelling and associate with the deaf rather than his hearing peers.

The social implications of those who are classified as *totally deaf and unable to speak* are many. In fact, they are too numerous to mention. However, a few are so marked and noticeable that they should be reviewed. These individuals live in a *structured world of the deaf.* All their social activities involve their participation with only deaf participants. They attend only sport activities that are organized and supervised by the deaf and include only deaf athletes. Whether it is bowling, basketball or other activities, the leading role is played by or carried on by the deaf, only. Rarely will they be seen at a sports event where the participants have normal hearing. This so-called clannishness is denied but nevertheless holds true. They attend the church for the deaf, the club for the deaf, the picnic for the deaf but refrain from other types of group activities. It is here that they are most likely to feel comfortable in their environment and make the better social adjustment. They have little or no association with orally speaking deaf, hard of hearing, or hearing handicapped individuals. Usually they marry individuals with similar ideas and conceptions and the carry over to their children is pretty much the same for much of their lives. The exception is when the children have normal hearing and eventually break away from the home environment. These individuals contribute little to society in general; nor do they add to the image of the totally deaf as a whole. Personality wise, they appear as unhappy people, disgruntled, lacking in humor, rarely smiling and overall provide the impression as strange people! The above statements will, in all probability, be rejected by some leaders of the deaf and shouts of unfair, etc. will be directed to this writer's remarks; however, they will admit that much of what was said is only too true and applies to too many of the unsociable deaf that exist in our society.

Those of the totally deaf group who have learned to speak and yet refuse to speak, too, have their social hang ups. Many of the earlier statements apply also to this group.

Very vividly, this author remembers many deaf individuals who had been taught to speak and have had very good deaf speech but refused to use it. Once he gained the ability to communicate in finger spelling and sign language he ceased using his speech. Even though he could communicate with hearing people by voice, he would persist in using manualism. The core of this behavior is associated with unpleasant memories going back to his childhood. Somewhere during the developmental growth of the individual while learning oralism he was not indoctrinated or prepared to realize and accept the fact that even though he moved his mouth and produced sounds, these noises that he ejected were not in any proportion acceptable to society. The odd expressions, embarrassments, flushing and behavior of normal hearing society to his vocalizations resulted in his sudden realization that his speech must be pretty poor and to such an extent that his hearing peers reacted strangely to his attempts of phonation. His former teachers, parents, family and close associates could understand him without too much difficulty. But nowhere was he conditioned or forewarned that society in general had not been prepared to listen to him. Thus he slowly closed the door to oral communication and instead resorted to the old standby—pencil and pad. Or, he too, limits himself to the world of the deaf in his social activities. I could not prove statistically the degree of clannishness in comparison with the first group. However, I am of the opinion from many years of experience and contact that the latter group tends to have less *standoffishness* and makes more effort to be a part of the community. He, too, is deaf oriented to certain activities pertaining to his social habits;

however, he will try to associate more in the so-called *hearing world.*

The totally deaf oralist is more socially oriented and disclaims any association with the undesirable, gesture making, hand talking deaf population. *I am an oralist!* However, here too, although he strives to be active in community affairs and is active to a degree, a close check reveals that his social outlets are almost always and only with others who are deaf oralists. Once leaving the school environment of easy communication, he finds that people just don't articulate speech as clearly as in the sheltered training grounds. With his good deaf speech, he is soon easily understood; however, receiving the question, answer or message back is something else to be desired. Then too, his hearing aid presents a false picture of his communication ability, since he has little residual hearing for speech. Most of the lay public is under the impression that hearing aids enable everybody to hear! This group being discussed use hearing aids primarily to keep them in the world of sound and not silence. Many of these individuals, too, develop undesirable characteristics, namely—they are *pretenders!* They pretend to understand, smile and nod their heads and have not the slightest idea of what is being said. They also resent assistance in communication and violently so. Furthermore, if offered a pad with a written message, they will tear it up or throw it into a person's face. Many times they are as unrealistic as to make such a statement, "I am glad that I was born deaf!" Overall, they move about in the hearing world with their pecularities. Some, in spite of the above, are very active in community affairs especially if their spouse has normal hearing and plays the role of special communicator. However, a large number become very lonesome and disenchanted with oralism as a means of communication. Slowly but surely they eventually seek out the deaf groups that use manualism as their means of communication. This opens up a new world of friendships, social activities and ease in understanding. The welcome relief from the tension of straining to read lips and being able to communicate through signs and finger spelling has opened up a new life for many many oralists.

The deafened present the most tragic picture of inadequacy insofar as adjustment to their social environment, once they have lost all of their hearing. With slow recovery from their illness or accident that causes the hearing impairment, there is even a greater psychological shock to the emotional system with the realization that nothing can be done to restore their hearing function. We are speaking here about those individuals who have a sudden onset of complete bilateral deafness. Amplification may be of some help to those who have a small amount of residual hearing and are not totally deaf, but nevertheless have very little discrimination ability. Usually their only recourse for communication is lip reading or the traditional pencil and pad. All socialization comes to a standstill as they grope for competing communication signals to help them interpret the spoken word. Intensive lip reading therapy and great efforts on the part of the family is of some value to too few. The causation factor of the deafness, too, plays an indirect role in whether or not they will become fair or good lip readers. Age, also, plays a role in progress toward becoming a skilled speech reader. Many of these individuals eventually seek the world of the sign language communicator and are slowly emerged and become socially accepted and to a degree, find happiness.

The hard of hearing have the least problem in adjusting to social situations once they have realistically accepted their problem and make use of amplification. The *psyche hump,* if such a thing exists, is the barrier that permits a realistic adjustment versus unrealistic adjustment in normal society. Of course, many can have corrected middle ear surgery and once again are transported into normal hearing society. Many of the neurotic symptoms in their behavior makeup then slowly, but surely, disappear. The literature is filled with success stories of those who have experienced these manifestations. Leagues and societies for the hard of hearing played a major role in social rehabilitation twenty-five to thirty years ago. Rightfully so, their function was to provide a place for hard of hearing individuals to congregate, exchange stories of distress, learn lip reading, play cards, watch movies, etc. Most of these hard of hearing individuals had more than a mild loss of hearing and needed such a social environment to supplement and support their mores. Today, with amplification, and effort, and will to do so, most hard of hearing individuals can and should participate in normal hearing society. Their active roles should be directed towards acceptance and use of their many talents within the community.

The hard of hearing signer finds himself happy in the social world of manualism. Although he has a decided problem in hearing, he has little difficulty in communicating because all his friends are manualists and deaf. Many times he is called on to play the role of interpreter in certain situations and this adds to his prestige as a needed individual. All of us experience elated feelings when we feel needed and can do for others. Rarely does the hard of hearing signer accept and use amplification. Of course there are exceptions to the rule but for the most part they prefer to be non-communicative auditorily. Their speech is typically slurred, distorted and demonstrates a hearing inadequacy. Nevertheless, it is understandable and used to some extent in certain situations. His social activities as previously mentioned are deaf oriented and here is where he is comfortable and at ease. If he seeks a wife or vice versa, a husband, the individual in most cases will find a totally deaf partner. Most of the time, these marriages work out very well and result in successful relationships. For further clarification, the reader must remember that this writer indicated that these individuals were educated in schools for the deaf where the above patterns of behavior and communication were developed.

The vocational implications as associated with the terminology expressed above leaves much to the imagination. The lack of communication oral by the totally deaf limits them considerably in finding suitable occupations. We hear consistently that they are under-employed, etc. We hear too, that educationally and vocationally they are inadequately trained and performing far below their true level of achievement. Employers and directors of training institutions (vocational) have for years shied away from accepting the above named disabled group because of the difficulty in providing instruction, assignment of responsibilities, lack of understanding of deafness, safety, and other sundry items. The lay public in general still see them as *deaf mutes, deaf and dumb, peculiar* people, and other undesirable classifications. As a former rehabilitation specialist for the deaf, this writer consistently was faced with the dilemma of convincing employers and training agencies to accept and provide opportunities for services. There is also a feeling of uneasiness on the part of society in general in associating and mixing with the totally deaf. Rehabilitation counselors, themselves, have expressed qualms about being in their company due to the communication barrier. More and more, we see the spread of different types of media to enlighten the public toward accepting the sign-making or communicating idea. More and more, organizations for and by the deaf, are spreading the *gospel* on community activities as an integral function and responsibility of deaf people. Nationally, classes for learning sign language and manualism by normal hearing society are being promoted and encouraged. All this is good for the deaf and for the community.

The totally deaf individual who has acquired speech, even though it is poor speech, must change his attitude toward the use of same. He must somehow be counseled into realizing that his potential for bettering himself vocationally rests with his acceptance and use of his tools of communicating. Whoever works with him toward a training or placement opportunity should be aware of the communication asset and use same as a part of the bit in selling his client's product. If an employer realizes that John or Mary can say, *No, Yes, I don't think so!* and other short statements, his resistance to employ an individual begins to break down. Also his reluctance against *mutism* begins to deteriorate, and he is more apt to consider the fairness of providing a trial or opportunity. Within the training or employment environments, this ability for some speech provides for a better relationship and easier associations.

The totally deaf oralist has much to learn about improving his personality and overall attitudes concerning his communication problem. In most cases, he is superior in overall knowledge and language development. He usually seeks and obtains white collar employment. He may have had several years of college training, and this has been in a regular college, rather than the one or two that are now in existence for the sign language communicating totally deaf. By and large, he is quite successful in his employment situation and especially if he initially has had some vocational training relating to his occupation. Counseling with the deaf oralist needs to be directed toward helping him remove some of the unfavorable obsessions as originally described previously under *social implications.* His realistic acceptance of all types of communication *helps* will do much to make him a well adjusted individual within his vocational environment. By the same token, too, he must rid himself or alleviate his thinking processes as to the personification of the deaf. Nearby associates must be made aware of the fact that the pseudo hearing aids are providing sounds to the individual; but not functional hearing. Again, counseling plays the leading role in helping individuals to be individuals and not miscellaneous apprehensive freaks.

The deafened are the pitiful group that have undergone trauma, shock, illness and sudden realization that one of their most precious senses has been taken away from them. Counseling and guidance toward acceptance is the major role for the audiologist, psychologist, otologist and rehabilitation counselor. Even though he may be able to return to his previous employment a lot of *spade work* has to be done to help him realistically adjust to his handicap. The three psychological levels of hearing functions according to Ramsdell (1960) are suddenly withdrawn from this individual. The sudden incidence of *silence* after years of normal hearing function must be shattering to the *psyche.* Immediate and specialized techniques of lip reading training are a must and these have to be diverted toward obtaining the best cooperation on the part of all individuals who have contact with the individual. Vocational planning for those who cannot return to their former occupations must be thought of in terms of related fields in order to make use of the skills the person has to keep up morale. The question which stands out now is, "How can we provide training that is related and make use of interests as well as skills?" Emphatically, vocational training and placement should not be directed toward, *where can he perform or be employed that will not require hearing?* Yes, special concessions will have to be made at times for the severe communication obstruction; however, these will become less and less as the individual strives to become a well adjusted deafened individual.

The vocational potentials of the hard of hearing are unlimited (depending, of course, upon mental capabilities, attitudes, realistic acceptance of hearing disability and the efforts made toward improving communication skills). Repeatedly, this writer has said to his graduate students in rehabilitation audiology, that hearing disabilities *make* some individuals and devastate others. This thinking too, applies to families of all handicapped individuals. Some people allow there being a handicapped member in the family destroy them as individuals, while others achieve promethean heights and excel beyond all expectations as citizens within a community. Hard of hearing persons are sure of services to aid them communicatively and realistically toward successful careers. They must admit their physical limitations and demonstrate evidence of doing everything possible to reduce the problem while working toward attainment of specific goals. We have in our society hard of hearing physicians, dentists, engineers, audiologists, and many others who are achieving success socially as well as vocationally. The challenge is up to the individual, he must face the fight and work upward continuously.

The hard of hearing signer often limits himself to lower vocational goals as a result of his educational and vocational training in residential schools for the deaf. Although there is no doubt that attempts were made to inspire him to achieve greater heights vocationally, his early age, plus lack of realization of the essence of education and its necessary implications prevent him from striving toward greater potential. Communicatively, he is more comfortable with the sign making deaf, and this too lowers his selection of challenging vocations. Of course, these statements do not apply to all hard of hearing signers, but unfortunately do apply to too many who would have and could have done better vocationally. Their rejection of amplification as a necessary communication adjunct also prevents attaining and working toward a higher goal. When later vocational opportunities become available, it is usually too late to change, due to family responsibilities and lack of necessary educational background, etc. Unfortunately, too many hard of hearing individuals are accepted into state residential schools for the deaf for their early training; however, since we have never provided schools for hard of hearing children or special school programs to handle these individuals, state superintendents have had no other choice other than to accept and offer their best programs to these individuals.

These ideas and expressions pertaining to the hearing impaired are the sole responsibility and thinking of this writer. The origination and development of this material has been implemented based first on his own hearing loss from age seven; then his thirty-seven years experience as a supervisor, teacher of the deaf, rehabilitation specialist for the deaf and hard of hearing and professor of audiology in a medical institution. Any critical indications are meant to be constructive in nature in order to provoke thinking.

REFERENCES

Davis, Hallowell and Silverman, S. Richard, Eds.: *Hearing and Deafness,* Rev Ed. New York: Holt, Rinehart & Winston, Inc., 1960.

Ramsdell, D. A.: The psychology of the hard of hearing and the deafened adult. In *Hearing and Deafness,* Hallowell Davis and S. Richard Silverman (Eds.). New York: Holt, Rinehart & Winston, Inc., 1960, p. 459.

Chapter V

DEAFNESS AND ITS EFFECTS

ANN GLASS

WHEN I STARTED TO WORK with deaf and hard of hearing persons in 1967 I had no idea of the extent of their exclusion from society. After a short time it become clear that they were given second class citizenship. They were shortchanged in education, ignored or downgraded in employment, tolerated in society, and often buffooned in the theatre. They were looked upon, in general, as not only without hearing, but without mind; deaf and dumb. All of the language I had heard for years came into focus, such as when children don't respond, "Are you deaf and dumb?," or "Hey, dummy" or "What's the matter, stupid. Can't you hear?" So these notions kept deaf persons a group apart from the hearing world. They were forced to form their own segregated groups where they could not only be understood but could find refuge from the stares, often condescending, of hearing persons.

I was and am distressed to observe that not only do hearing non-professionals stereotype deaf persons as a group, but so do the professional workers. I am aware that we all short-cut communication. However, it seems strange to me that among professionals working in the field of deafness, hearing handicapped persons are lumped together as *the deaf, the hard of hearing.* Although persons with hearing loss, total or partial, are all individuals, they are viewed, at least in the term describing them, as a type or species. This terminology, it seems to me, removes their individual differences and highlights only their sameness. As I see it, disabled persons, regardless of their medical condition are persons who happen to have some physical, mental, or emotional deviation which causes them particular problems. To me, it is a mistake to speak of *the deaf, the hard of hearing, the blind, the mentally retarded,* etc. As I stated previously, I'm sure this is all done for quick identification, but I think it identifies and reinforces the weaknesses instead of the strengths.

What is inherent in the physical disability and what is caused by other factors? Mentally retarded persons are the way they are because of certain inherent limitations of their intellectual capacities. They are able to achieve up to a limited level only. There is a ceiling on the amount of information they can assimilate. The mental condition itself, therefore, is the handicap.

With blind persons we have learned that the absence or limitation of vision, in and of itself, does not have within it barriers to learning and training for work. It has been shown, over and over again, that with proper training, first mobility, then educational or vocational, blind persons can become functioning and contributing members of society. It has been demonstrated that they can achieve high goals and that there is a wide range of ability, just as there is in the general population.

Little by little, progress is being made in the understanding about deaf persons. There is little inherent in the disability that creates the problems. It is the lack of services because of our lack of understanding that creates the problems.

There are some basic principles of human behavior that are pertinent to attitudes toward hearing handicapped persons. When we address someone, we expect a response. If no response is forthcoming, we make several assumptions: 1) he is ignoring us; this infuriates us; 2) he doesn't understand us; this makes us uncomfortable and anxious. The methods we have of handling our own feelings are: 1) to get even, 2) to relieve our own anxiety by leaving the scene. It never occurs to most of us that perhaps the person may just not have been able to hear us. Maybe his language understanding does not include the words we have employed.

An interesting commentary is, that if we were traveling in a foreign country and spoke to a native, we would: 1) try to learn something of his language, 2) repeat in a way he might understand, perhaps by gesture, 3) look for an interpreter.

Until now the above has not applied to our contacts with deaf persons. We have avoided them, whenever possible. If we have been unable to avoid them, as in professional contacts, we have done whatever has been the easiest, avoided communication. We have categorized them as uninterested or non-motivated if they have objected to our techniques. Those who are compliant are placed in jobs far beneath their capacities.

There is a basic difference between deaf persons and foreigners. In a foreign country, the visitor is the stranger and he must make the effort to be understood. Also, it is quite obvious that there is a language barrier. Deafness does not show. The person looks like everyone else. In our verbal society, we judge people by what they say. We often give meaning to what we hear beyond the actual words themselves. We interpret noises we hear in light of our moods or our moods are created by the sounds we hear. Our listeners respond to what we say by doing certain things, responding to our speech in like manner, or making certain facial expressions.

A person with a hearing loss is denied this kind of interchange. He cannot hear the words; therefore, he cannot respond in the expected fashion; whether it be to do what is requested or to answer a question. He is unable even to make the appropriate facial grimaces. He is, in essence, looking at a blank wall and responding to it, in kind, blankly. He may defend his inadequacy by smiling, because he knows a smile is a sure indicator of friendliness. The conversation may not intend to elicit a smile; this is unknown to him. His smile, he hopes, will satisfy the speaker in some way. It serves often only to categorize him as *stupid.*

Because deafness is invisible, to all intents and purposes, it does not exist. The human tendency is to avert one's eyes from something one wants to avoid. This is not necessary in dealing with deaf persons. We don't have to use the mechanism *out of sight–out of mind.* If the individual is hard of hearing and wearing a hearing aid, we know something is the matter, but in our mechanistic orientation, it seems only necessary to turn it on or up, and everything will be OK.

Many hearing handicapped persons themselves reinforce the view of the hearing population. They depend upon lip reading for understanding. It has been estimated that only 23 per cent of the population can learn to speech read effectively. Those few manage to get along. The others guess at what is said and though they feel they are part of the hearing world, they are not. There are several ways deaf people see and group themselves. They either try to align themselves with the hearing population, and by refusing to use manual communication, they think they are part of the hearing population. They may go to the other extreme and associate only with other deaf persons. They can accept themselves as deaf or hard of hearing, thereby gaining status in their own groups and also having a place in hearing groups. The latter approach has to be a two way interaction. It is not possible as long as suspicion and disrespect are present.

All of the above shows how little understanding exists about deafness. There is disagreement even among experts about the thinking processes of deaf people. For some time, the opinion was that all deaf persons were intellectually slower than hearing persons. This was based on the results of verbal tests validated on hearing persons with language. Furthermore, these tests were administered by testers who had no experience in testing deaf persons. Also the tests were group tests and not suitable for deaf persons who need to be tested individually, or at least given individual instructions. Myklebust and Levine, psychologists with experience in dealing with deaf persons tried non-verbal material and reached the conclusion that when suitable test instruments were used in suitable conditions, *deaf persons displayed the same range of abilities as everyone else*. At Oregon State School for the Deaf, it was demonstrated by Doctor Bannich that when each student was tested non-verbally, there was the same range of differences as among hearing people. Hans Furth, Catholic University, Washington, D. C., came up with the same conclusion. The consensus was that deaf persons were like everyone else except they had communication problems.

Ever so gradually there has been developing an interest and concern for that part of our population with hearing disabilities. It has been necessary to define deafness and to consider the age of onset. The age of onset is important to begin assessment of individual's development of language. We need to know the kind of hearing impairment, the nature and extent of other organic defects, the environment in which the individual lives and his education.

To begin to assess deaf children's aptitudes and interests, work and thought is being given to identification of suitable instruments. Some of the prevailing instruments were found useful for typical groups in specific ways. To be valid for a deaf child, the instrument must be non-verbal for there has been no development of speech and language or there has been little increase in language understanding, and verbal tests are not fair or valid. Verbal tests with deaf children measure language deficiency due to hearing loss rather than measuring intelligence. There have been innumerable cases of people, whose major problem is deafness, being sent to institutions for retarded persons on the basis of low test scores. Even some non-verbal tests are not appropriate because they require verbal directions. Hard of hearing children may give the impression of being able to understand verbal tests, but this is often an artifice. It is advisable to begin these children with a performance test and then, if desired, a verbal instrument may be tried. In cases where the performance score is appreciably higher, the probability is that the lower score on the test involving language is due to hearing impairment and does not constitute a true measure of intelligence.

The employer group, as a whole, has had little contact with deaf persons. This is due to the communication barrier and the time consumption of using writing for transmission of information. Employers need to be convinced that people can learn by written message and by demonstration. One of the best means of convincing them is to point out the employment record of hearing-handicapped workers. It may be worthwhile to an employer to avoid excessive and expensive turnover by spending extra time training a deaf worker who will be a responsible and loyal employee. It is up to the schools for deaf children and special education programs to teach job responsibility and loyalty.

The general problems a deaf person faces when he applies

for work are many. They are the immediate communication lack, the employer's long standing attitudes regarding deafness created by past experiences with deaf persons and by prejudice, lack of social understanding and technical ability.

Like all workers, a deaf worker's continued employment and job advancement depend on his ability to perform his entry job well and to respond to training. Unlike others, however, he has the additional obligation to develop a means of communication with his shop boss and fellow workers.

Educators of deaf children need to emphasize employee roles and responsibilities, and to acquaint them with the world as it is, not as it looks.

Even a trained, well-adjusted deaf person runs into stumbling blocks. Unprepared and inexperienced deaf job seekers have even more difficulty. The vocational programs in schools for the deaf are not complete or up-to-date. The graduate goes out into the labor market poorly prepared, educationally retarded, and socially inept.

He may try to apply for work accompanied by a hearing individual. Sometimes this serves only to raise questions about his *self-sufficiency*. His inability to fill out application forms reinforces notions that he is mentally slow. His inability to read and interpret test instructions will handicap him in taking written job knowledge or aptitude and intelligence tests. The job interview, itself, will be an obstacle.

Lack of skill in applying for a job, deficiency in entry work skills, inadequate written language, lack of functional oral language all serve to bar a deaf applicant from employment. Job hunting techniques need to be taught in schools for the deaf and special education programs for the hearing handicapped. How to dress, how to present one's self to a receptionist, how to complete an application, how to write a résumé, and how to present it, are all facets of securing employment.

The job résumé needs to include an initial statement explaining the individual as deaf and is seeking work. If he lip reads, he should indicate this and explain the suitable conditions to accomplish this. This should be followed by personal data, educational and vocational training, work experience, hobbies and interests. This should be taught as a supplement to vocational training.

Also, schools need to expose graduates to personnel, aptitude, and job knowledge tests, and to acquaint them with test-taking techniques.

The students could also be given experience in interviewing prospective employers by role-playing sessions in school. The stumbling blocks in job hunting are known. We need to prepare students for them.

After an individual is placed, adjustment problems may become evident. For deaf persons, these are often more extreme because of the communication barrier. The lack of understanding and knowledge about job loyalty and responsibility are barriers to continued employment and promotion. These need to be explored and explained as part of the vocational training program. Teaching skills are not enough. Work attitudes are equally important. Good work attitudes often are more important than great skill. An employer will often overlook an individual's lack of skill, if he likes the individual. He may even take time to teach him in order to retain him in the organization.

The greatest single problem on the job does not seem to be the deaf person's acquisition of job skills. It hinges, rather, on his erratic work habits and, often, anti-social behavior. Schools need to enlarge their curricula to include courses on responsibility of an employee to an employer. There needs to be increased communication between schools and employers.

We define rehabilitation as the *restoration of an individual to the maximum level of social, emotional, and vocational functioning of which he is capable.* In the case of many deaf persons, it is *habilitation* because they are not to be *restored* but *started* on the way toward functioning. For those who are hard of hearing, this is also true; for many of them have never been given the opportunity to exercise their maximum functioning. Instead of their ability, it has been their disability that has been emphasized. Unlike the popular song, we have *accentuated the negative and eliminated the positive.*

The progress that is being made by hearing handicapped persons aided by hearing individuals is encouraging. Deaf workers, in general, have a good record. Their counterparts among hearing persons leave jobs because they want a *voice* in the management. A *foot in the door* is what deaf people want. The door is gradually being pushed open. Hopefully, deaf persons will be allowed to get to the top floor.

The California Department of Rehabilitation became concerned over its lack of personnel able to communicate with deaf persons. For some time there were only two counselors for deaf persons, one in Northern California and one in Southern California. In 1963 the Department, newly formed under its own director, began an active program to assign counselors to specialize with hearing handicapped persons. These counselors were provided with training in sign language and courses related to the psychology of deafness and special problems encountered by deaf persons.

These counselors received all of the deaf and hard of hearing applicants and built up a case load of these persons. It was interesting to observe that many deaf persons had previously been denied services on the basis they were employed and, therefore, had no vocational handicap. When they saw a counselor who understood them, could communicate with them, and who realized that they were definitely underemployed, their cases were reopened and necessary training provided for more suitable occupations. The counselors for deaf and hard of hearing persons embarked upon a community education program enlightening as many persons as possible to the abilities of deaf people. The counselors also learned more about their own communities, becoming acquainted with hearing persons involved with deaf persons and able to communicate with them. Thus, people who could be used as interpreters, tutors and aides were found. The counselors also learned about social, church and educational resources for their clients. Not only did deaf persons benefit, but so did the counselors whose horizons had expanded.

Currently there are special counselors for hearing handicapped persons in each rehabilitation district of the state. Some of them have secretaries and aides who know sign language. There is also a full time coordinator of services to deaf persons on the central office staff.

The following are case studies from my case load. Some individuals have achieved and some have not. The reasons are not clear but good family relationships seem to contribute to individuals' feelings of self worth.

Case A

In 1969, a short, poorly dressed and ill kept man of thirty-three appeared at the Los Angeles office of the Department of Rehabilitation writing down, "I am deaf—need job and money." He indicated he had a place to stay, was vague about where he'd come from but insisted he would work if he had suitable training. He was referred to the counselor for the deaf who communicated in sign language. She determined he had gone to a school for the deaf to the tenth grade and had quit. He reported he was divorced and his wife had custody of their child who was six years old at that time. He asked for training in body and fender repair and seemed motivated, so was enrolled in a trade school in Los Angeles. He gave every indication of having been a floater but seemed interested in settling down.

He was referred to welfare by the vocational rehabilitation counselor and he was housed in the unattached men's service center. Because the welfare process was slow, vocational rehabilitation provided maintenance and transportation as well as training fees and purchased tools for him during training. The training plan was to be of twenty-eight weeks duration at a cost of:

Training	$1,090.00
Tools	410.22
Transportation	117.04
Maintenance	475.00
Total	$2,092.26

The week he started, he missed several days due to abdominal complaints. He returned after a few days and then missed again, reporting he'd been involved in an auto accident. He did not return to school and in the meantime, the school closed and it became necessary to secure another training resource. The rehabilitation counselor took him to various shops to try to analyze on-the-job training. A shop was located which agreed to pay a wage to him as a regular employee. He requested and was given additional tools from the agency stockroom and others were purchased amounting to $149. He accepted all the tools but worked only one week saying he'd been laid off because he had a back problem and was unable to do the work. He kept the tools saying he expected to return to work when his condition improved. He did not return to work. Instead he applied for welfare insisting still that this was temporary. A month later he was hired by a body and fender man who knew sign language. He was arrested the next day for begging on the street. The employer still decided to take him back, however.

A week later the man was fired because of excessive absences and drinking on the job. He was picked up for vagrancy several times. Efforts were made to get our tools back, but it was learned the man had moved, leaving no forwarding address.

He returned sometime later saying he'd been ill and in need of hospitalization. He also spoke of a possible job where he would use the tools. Instead of going to work he went to jail for vagrancy. While in jail, he wrote the name of his rehabilitation counselor and she was called to the Women's Probation Department where the man was being held for impersonation.

He then disappeared with the tools and a year later appeared at the Sacramento, California office. Efforts were made to get the tools back but the man reported they'd been stolen. He asked for more tools but was told none would be issued until he secured work which could be verified.

Because of his poor past record I couldn't recommend him to employers. He receives Aid to the Disabled of $140 per month. He keeps saying he wants a job but it is questionable he will get one.

Medical Information. This man has a severe congenital bilateral sensori-neural hearing loss. Only speech awareness thresholds could be established since he could distinguish no test words. A hearing aid was purchased for him as one seemed helpful but he never wore it.

Case B

Mr. B., an engineer, and his wife who is a college graduate and whose main goal in life was to be a mother and wife, enjoyed their two lovely blonde children, a girl and boy, three years apart in age. Mrs. B. spent all of her time with them, making up games and songs and enjoying their wide-eyed appreciation. Their playmates were involved with them and the B.'s home was the *fun-place* of the block.

In 1950 when the little girl was three, the family decided to spend Thanksgiving in Los Angeles with good friends. The little girl's birthday was to be celebrated that same week. Preparations for the trip were made excitedly and in great anticipation. The day before departure the little girl suddenly complained of a very sore nape of the neck. The family pediatrician was called and he ordered a spinal tap. This test was negative but the child's fever zoomed and she went into a coma. She was immediately hospitalized and a diagnosis of influenzal meningitis was made. Medication was instantly prescribed. The child was in a coma about three days and in the hospital nineteen. As soon as she came out of the coma, her mother realized the child had lost her hearing. She also had no balance and could not walk. She was extremely fearful and clung to her mother and father when they visited. The mother was permitted to be with her constantly.

When the child came home her parents devoted all of their time to her. They gave up their social activities, played with her constantly and were with her through her waking hours and sat near her until they were sure she was fast asleep.

The mother continued her activities and spoke to the child as she had before, using familiar words and introducing new ones as the situation demanded them. The child had always been precocious and had spoken early so she had a considerable vocabulary to start with.

The child's walking ability did not return for one year and it took about one and a half years for her to regain her confidence in herself and her trust in others. The parents took her to a speech and hearing clinic to try to learn how to communicate better with her. While there, they learned of the John Tracy Clinic in Southern California and its program to teach lip reading to hearing impaired persons.

The family applied and was accepted for the summer program. The mother and two children stayed for six weeks. The father was able to come only during his two weeks vacation period. The family learned about speech reading and the child's trust and self-confidence increased. The rest of the family became more confident and lost some of their helpless feeling. Their pattern of doing things together continued. There had never been any recrimination about the situation, as all that could be done had been done. The parents were extremely supportive of each other, as they had always been. The children received as much attention, if not more, as they always had. The little boy was not neglected. He was involved in a family situation and was a very important factor in it.

When the child was four a special class was set up in a school away from her neighborhood in which there were three other deaf children. The child was accepted as a five year old as she was advanced. At about this time the parents discussed the mother's eligibility for a teaching credential and made plans for her to secure it. She had demonstrated her ability by working with her own and other deaf children as she had volunteered in the special class. She realized her responsibility to deaf children but before going ahead for a credential she and her husband discussed the unsuitability of their child being in a school away from her neighborhood and friends. They were able, therefore, to have her accepted in the neighborhood school where she went one hour each morning, after going to the other school. She stayed in neighborhood schools throughout her school years, never going to special classes. She was graduated from a regular high school where she made excellent grades. She wore binaural hearing aids which brought in no speech but only sounds. She sat in front where she could read the teachers' lips and was well adjusted.

She had many friends and became a junior hospital volunteer, a Peppermint. She soon was president of that organization. In that position she had to do a great deal of telephone communication. Her parents had heard of a special telephone in which the earphone and the mouthpiece are separate. They secured one and when the phone rang, the mother listened to the message, spoke it to the girl who gave the answer herself. She, therefore, used her voice all the time and preserved its quality. Part of her job was to be involved with the Children's Hospital and her colleagues as well as her mother assisted with the telephone procedure.

Because of her hospital involvement she became interested in nursing and selected a small Catholic college in San Francisco to attend. Her parents realized she could not be a nurse without a hearing associate always at her side; but the girl insisted. Before she started to college, however, the head of nursing confirmed the parents' advice and the girl changed to a journalism and later to an English major. The Department of Rehabilitation underwrote her college plan though ordinarily private colleges are not used. The family had made such an intensive study of the value of a small intimate college to the girl, however, that it was allowed. The agency paid also for notetaker services to allow other students to take and go over notes for the girl. She, herself, in her self-assured way talked to the instructors, many of whom loaned her their own notes to study or gave her additional material to work on. She secured her B.A. in June, 1971.

In the meantime at a girl friend's house she met a young man and fell in love. She decided to get whatever work she could and live at home to save money. She secured work as a clerk typist for the state and is saving her money toward marriage. Her fiancé is in the service and hopes to go to school upon discharge.

Her mother, in the meantime, has become an expert on speechreading and is a consultant in the field of cued speech for the school district. She works full time as an elementary school teacher.

The family relationship is a close one with all members being respected and well regarded. The girl's accomplishments are due greatly to this as well as to her native ability.

Case C

Mr. and Mrs. G. had been married for twenty years without having children. Mrs. G. then conceived and with great joy produced a son. He was handsome and cheerful but somehow, unresponsive. It was not until he was two that his deafness was revealed. Up until that point he had been viewed as a slow learner. His parents kept him in the house fearful that he would get hurt. He had no friends and spent time only in the house. He had no speech. His mother mouthed to him and pointed out what she meant but he did not learn to lip read; he only followed her motions and actions.

When it was time for him to go to school his parents tentatively enrolled him at the California School for the Deaf in Berkeley, California. They allowed him to stay a very short time as they *worried about him* and brought him home. He was enrolled in day school but could not get along and there were no aurally handicapped classes at that time. John then stayed at home playing alone or with his mother.

When he was twenty-one he went to work as a laborer in a mattress factory at a very low wage. He then went to work as a laborer in a smoke house leaving that for another labor job. He worked at labor until 1951 when his parents bought a motel in Idaho and he worked as janitor and yardman. His parents stayed in the motel business until they retired in 1969 and John helped them.

John was committed to a state mental institution in 1956 and 1957 when he developed a chronic drinking problem and became hostile and difficult to manage. He was discharged to his parents and stayed at home for the next two years. In 1959 he was recommitted with a diagnosis of sociopathic personality disturbance and alcoholism. He remained in the hospital one year and again returned home. He was recommitted one year later remaining in the hospital for two years, then placed on day care under supervision of his parents. He was discharged from the hospital three years later and referred to a psychiatric social worker who referred him to vocational rehabilitation.

At our first contact, John used rudimentary sign language,

mostly home-made signs. His mother seemed distressed that she was left out of the conversation. She kept interjecting her own conversational technique of mouthing and pointing. It was very apparent that John needed association with other deaf people. I asked a deaf man to visit him and interest him in coming to the deaf club. John's mother discouraged this. Though she did not say so, her concern seemed to be related to her fear of her son's drinking problem. His behavior since his discharge from the hospital has been good but he has been at home all of the time and watched by her. She spoke of electronic assembly as a good field for him as he had good manual dexterity. I learned that the San Jose Goodwill had contracts from Lockheed and was doing training on electronic assembly. John's mother, who did all of the negotiating for him, felt this would be a good spot for him. They were given a transportation allowance and the mother drove them to San Jose. John has no driver's license because of his drinking history. When they returned, the mother and John expressed satisfaction with the training but decided against moving to San Jose as John's father was ailing and getting worse. The mother decided nothing should be done at that time and we closed our case.

Two years later the mother re-applied for help for her son. He had been struck by a hit and run driver and was in the hospital with mangled legs and there was some question of his mobility upon recovery. He also had a badly lacerated face and was scheduled for plastic surgery.

The parents were still operating a motel and their concern was about John's employability upon recovery. He had been helping around the motel but this would no longer be possible if his legs did not improve. It took six months for his casts to be removed and six more months for him to be out of a wheelchair. The mother insisted on our maintaining contact throughout this period and when John was out of the wheelchair he and his mother asked for training. I was willing to arrange a pre-vocational program but transportation presented a problem. The mother refused to allow John to get a driver's license and she could not transport him daily so again we closed our case.

Two years later the mother re-applied saying she and her husband had retired from the motel business and John needed work. Efforts were made to locate employment to no avail. The mother then decided to make some contacts of her own and the case was closed. Two years later the mother re-applied reporting her husband had died and she and her son were trying to adjust to this. The family income was Social Security for the mother, Social Security Disability and Aid to the Disabled for the son. He had been drawing this aid throughout our contact. The mother has become even more involved with him and though she speaks of worrying about his future, she places obstacles in the road of planning. By this time John was 51, had little communication ability and was a very dependent person. Unless we could secure work for him as a laborer, which he had done where communication was minimal we again would have to close his case. This is an example of a situation in which social services were required long ago to prepare this family for releasing John and allowing him to grow up.

Case D

Mr. W., a law student, married a secretary who worked to help put him through law school. After graduation from law school and just before he entered practice they decided to have children. Their first daughter was beautiful and responsive. Their second daughter was beautiful and non-responsive and it was discovered she was congenitally deaf due to Rubella that the mother suffered early in pregnancy. The parents spent time with their children, spoke to them both as if they could hear and were not hesitant about taking their deaf child with them wherever they went.

The marriage split up, however, due to incompatibility and the father remarried. The mother took in boarders so she could stay home with her children. As they grew up they helped her with the cleaning and cooking. The mother opened a board and care facility and the girls had much company.

The little deaf girl went to regular classes. She was well behaved and quiet and was ignored in class as *she was no trouble.* She then was placed in the aurally handicapped class in high school. She did unusually well, so well in fact that the question arose about the validity of her hearing loss. Otological exams confirmed a profound bilateral sensori-neural hearing loss with not enough residual hearing to conduct a speech discrimination test. She was, however, able to discriminate speech with visual clues. She had worn a hearing aid since early childhood.

She had no useable speech, knew no sign language and was a poor lip reader. She had fair command of language and could write understandably.

She was not referred to Department of Rehabilitation immediately from high school because of lack of interest. She came in on her own, however, a year later. She was sent to a local business college for a key punch training course. Upon completion a job was secured for her in San Francisco. She stayed six months and returned to Sacramento because she was lonely. Another job was found for her for the federal government. She did very well and began to mix with deaf people. She also learned sign language. She asked for and was given a transfer to Washington, D. C. so she could attend classes at Gallaudet College. She was taking classes and working and was named federal employee of the year at one time.

Case E

Robert is twenty-five. He has five hearing siblings and one deaf sister, Helene. He lost his hearing when he was two as a result of a high fever accompanying a case of the mumps. He had just started talking a great deal when he lost his hearing. The shock of his inability to hear was great on his parents but didn't seem to disturb his siblings and friends who continued to play with him and who soon developed a means of communication. His parents, too, after their initial shock developed a means of communication.

Two years later a baby girl was born deaf. The reason was never determined. The mother, having one deafened child and having had time to get used to this, did not feel too shocked, mainly startled. All of the children spent time with the baby enjoying her cuddliness and beauty. She learned to understand them. She, too, as she grew older, played with the neighborhood children.

Robert started school in his home community in a class for hearing handicapped children. This class was one morning per week. He was transferred to the California School for the Deaf in Berkeley at age seven and went there through high school. His sister started there at age five and went to the tenth grade dropping out to marry a classmate. She completed high school and secured her diploma from a home teacher after several years. Her husband, who was a drop out from the School for the Deaf, also completed his high school education after several years.

Robert, upon graduation, was referred to the Department of Rehabilitation counselor in his home district. He is an alert pleasant eager young man and at first was placed in a training program in an offset printing establishment. He had been in the print shop at the school. He did well, but the firm went out of business. He then was placed with several other deaf persons in a letter sorting position at the post office. Training was required first and an interpreter was paid to help in the training. Robert has been working over two years and is earning over three dollars per hour. He was married two years ago to a colleague from the School for the Deaf and she is a key punch operator for the state.

Helene's husband secured work in electronic assembly but he left the job and she and he moved to Sacramento to be near her family. They asked for help from the Department of Rehabilitation. Helene wanted training in typing and key punch. She was sent to business college but upon completion we could not find a job for her in key punch. Since she was a good seamstress and expressed interest in getting a job doing sewing, a job was secured for her in this field. After she worked six months at sewing, a key punch job was secured for her in the office where her sister-in-law works.

Her husband completed auto mechanic training under Rehabilitation sponsorship and we are now in the process of seeking work for him.

Chapter VI

DEAFNESS AND FAMILY PLANNING

CARL A. LARSON

IN THEIR MOST POIGNANT FORM problems of inheritance meet parents of congenitally deaf children. Since 40 per cent of all early and severe hearing impairment has hereditary causes such problems reach considerable social and economic dimensions. What parents wish to know is their risk of having a deaf child. This question can be put in somewhat different forms. Brothers and sisters of deaf persons may have apprehensions when planning to found a family, often enough they can be offered guidelines for their venture. Though simple facts of inheritance are well understood when explained to prospective parents, actual situations can seem to be tangled and require some additional comments.

Some family constellations may be difficult to explain by any hard and fast rule. Impaired hearing sometimes seems to run in a family without being inherited. In other kindreds deafness can be regularly and conspicuously inherited and then seem to go out of bounds in a single family. Then empirical knowledge about sources of deviations from expected proportions of children with and without impaired hearing can offer an explanation, or in some instances reasonably well founded alternative explanations, acceptable to prospective parents seeking advice.

WHAT IS INHERITED?

For all practical purposes the material basis of inheritance is chromosomal genes. A changed (mutant) gene has its site either in an X chromosome or in a chromosome not immediately concerned with the establishment of sex. The gene can be handed down from generation to generation regularly giving evidence of its presence, for instance by producing deafness, or concealed. Sometimes a few comments are needed to clarify the fact that deafness from extrinsic causes is not heritable. When explaining patterns of inheritance the counselor will find it useful to identify genes with factors of inheritance. Their presence or absence obeys simple rules of chance. It may, however, be well to remember that gene programs correspond to concrete chemical information. A mutant gene is a changed part of a DNA (deoxyribonucleic acid) molecule. In some instances it may be necessary to make clear that knowledge about the chemistry of the gene does not include precise information as to the composition of individual human genes. There is no way to identify deafness genes, as such, in normally hearing carriers.

AUTOSOMAL DOMINANT INHERITANCE

The Mendelian laws of inheritance are simple and readily understood. In midfrequency hearing loss an affected person has a parent who is likewise affected. Among brothers and sisters of patients 50 per cent have the same relatively mild form of deafness. When planning a family a man or a woman with midfrequency hearing loss has in prospect an equal number of affected and normally hearing children, provided that the spouse is free from this particular type of hearing defect. Behind this regular and predictable appearance of the anomaly lies the presence of the causative gene in an autosome, i.e., a chromosome not directly concerned with sex determination. Autosomes occur in pairs, in the type of defective hearing now discussed a child has an equal chance of carrying the harmless chromosome of its hard of hearing parent or the partner chromosome with the gene responsible for the hearing loss. In the latter case the child will reveal the same trait as the affected parent. Dominance implies that the presence of the mutant gene in one of the two matching chromosomes is enough to give rise to the anomaly.

The presence of the same trait in several family members in consecutive generations is typical of dominant inheritance. It is usually accepted by those immediately concerned as evidence of a heritable cause of the abnormality. As soon as the 50:50 chance of receiving the detrimental gene from an affected parent is well understood, family planning can be discussed on the basis of odds demonstrable by the flipping of coins. Only one of two companion chromosomes is handed down by the sex cell partaking in a given conception. Which one of them contributes to any subsequent conception is wholly independent of the first event. When an emotionally loaded family situation is discussed it may not be immediately clear to both parents of deaf children that the same 1:1, or 50 per cent, risk obtains for a following child after their having any number of deaf children. Again the demonstration of independent outcome of coin spinning after any series of foregoing trials will clarify the situation.

The question about children at risk can be formulated to concern not a particular child but the composition of a family. Given a gene for deafness, situated in one chromosome only of an autosomal pair, dominant inheritance implies the expectation of deafness in 50 per cent of the children of a man or woman

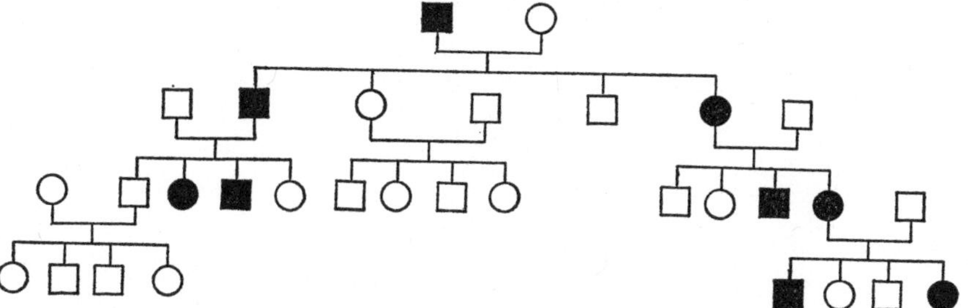

Figure VI-1. Autosomal dominant inheritance. Model pedigree. Squares: males; circles: females. Filled symbols: affected.

with this equipment. Nobody would expect four coins flipped to demonstrate this expectation to show, in each trial, one side twice and the other side twice. There will be chance deviations from the expected proportions. Thus a family of four children will, as readily demonstrated with the aid of four coins, be composed solely of hearing children in one instance of sixteen, while there is a one in sixteen risk of having four deaf children. The remaining fourteen possibilities are also included in the developed expression $(\frac{1}{2}D + \frac{1}{2}d)^4$, where, for instance, $\frac{4}{16}$ dd^3 implies a chance of $\frac{4}{16}$ of having a four-child family of one deaf and three hearing children (the deaf child taking any of the four positions, first to last, within the sibship).

While these rules are useful as basic precepts in family planning, most types of dominantly inherited deafness require some qualifications, to be discussed later. In general, the 50 per cent risk of having a deaf child under the circumstances mentioned here, is valid as a maximum figure for various types of deafness with an autosomal dominant mode of inheritance.

This type of transmission accounts for approximately 10 per cent of all congenital deafness. Typical families reveal bilateral hearing loss of 60 to 100 db in all affected members, with normal vestibular function. Other types of autosomal dominant deafness include high tone neural deafness with slow progression, a non-progressive, moderate to severe hearing loss often limited to one ear, and the midfrequency hearing loss already mentioned. A neural hearing decrement at 1000 and 2000 Hz, from 10 to about 50 dB, with slow progression, marks this type of hearing impairment. Otosclerosis and a series of syndromes (i.e. complexes of abnormalities) also belong to the autosomal dominant group of hearing difficulties.

AUTOSOMAL RECESSIVE INHERITANCE

Hearing impediments with recessive inheritance are not always conspicuously running in families. A deaf child often has hearing sibs and parents. An extensive family survey then reveals grandparents, uncles and aunts, cousins, nephews and nieces with no accountable impairment of hearing. Though this pattern is indeed typical of autosomal recessive inheritance, parents quite

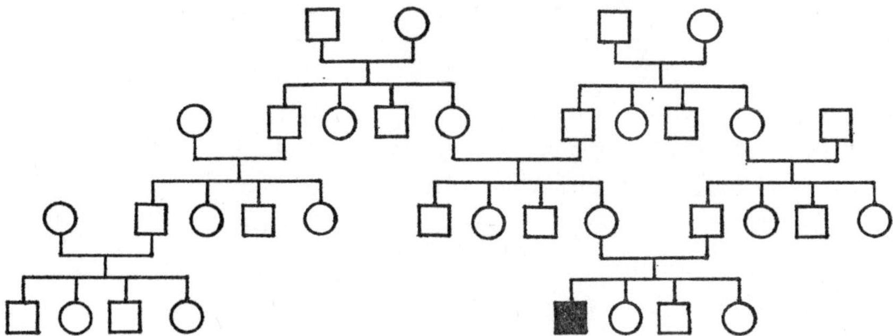

Figure VI-2. Autosomal recessive inheritance. Model pedigree. Symbols as in Figure VI-1.

naturally seek for other explanations. The material basis differs, however, not essentially from that of autosomal dominant inheritance. The mutant gene responsible for the hearing loss is carried by one member of a pair of homologous autosomes, mostly through a long array of generations. But the effects of this mutant gene come to the fore only in persons carrying the same gene in both partner chromosomes. Such persons have, as a rule, parents both carrying the same mutant gene in a single (heterozygous) dose.

In severe neural deafness (loss of 75 to 100 dB in all frequencies) with early onset some families have normally hearing parents and a single deaf child. In other families several children present this form of deafness, to be expected in $\frac{1}{4}$ of the children of two normally hearing gene carriers. For a simple demonstration of this risk a deck of playing cards can be used, the chance of having a deaf child equals the prospect of drawing a club. Chance deviations from expected proportions occur and can be explained to prospective parents. To illustrate, autosomal recessive inheritance is compatible with a four-child family of exclusively deaf children, the risk of this set amounting to 1 in 256. The prospect of four normally hearing children is $\frac{81}{256}$; these chances, as well as those of the remaining combinations, are accounted for by the expression $\left(\frac{3}{4}\text{H} + \frac{1}{4}\text{h}\right)^4$.

The general formula for any child number substitutes n for the exponent 4 (thus 3 for a 3-child family, 5 for a 5-child family etc.).

Brothers and sisters of persons with autosomal recessive deafness carry, when normally hearing, the detrimental gene in two instances of three. The risk of a given sib being a carrier is, in other words, $\frac{2}{3}$. As viewed from the angle of parents who are both hearing carriers the expected proportions are $\frac{1}{4}$ hearing non-carrier children, $\frac{2}{4}$ hearing carriers, $\frac{1}{4}$ deaf children. The first question was limited to the three hearing brothers and sisters, hence the carrier risk encountered in most real life situations. In normally motile populations this high risk, 66.7 per cent, still means a fairly low risk of having deaf children with a mate not belonging to the own kindred. Within small population groups where kin matings are relatively common, a deaf parent sometimes has a hearing mate carrying an identical detrimental gene. In such families 50 per cent of the children become deaf and all hearing children are gene carriers.

Carriers of mutant genes for impaired hearing are relatively common, but the risk of encountering a mating partner bearing the same damaging gene is of the order 1 per cent or less. The chance for the first cousin of an identified carrier of bearing the same gene, transmitted from a common grandparent, is precisely $\frac{1}{8}$, or 12.5 per cent. Only genes that occupy the same site in homologous chromosomes impair hearing by coming together in the same person. This explains the paradoxical situation when two parents, both with autosomal recessive deafness, have normally hearing children. Conversely, the identity of detrimental genes handed down within ethnic, religious or geographic isolates explain the sometimes exceptionally high frequency of recessive hearing disorder within such groups.

About 30 to 40 per cent of early, severe deafness is of autosomal recessive inheritance. This frequency estimate includes a number of incompletely known conditions with impaired hearing caused by different mutant genes, but also a considerable array of specific syndromes possible to identify by anomalies associated with the hearing defect.

SEX-LINKED INHERITANCE

Autosomal inheritance implies an even chance of males and females of being affected. For various reasons, more or less plain, one sex may be more frequently affected than the other. An excess of males need not exclude an autosomal gene as the cause of defective hearing, but in some families a neural hearing loss of 70 to 100 dB, involving all frequencies, occurs in sons of hearing mothers. In some instances this type of deafness, congenital, has been observed in brothers of carrier mothers.

This is the inheritance pattern of hemophilia, bleeder disease, to mention a classical representative of X-borne inheritance. A man carries one X chromosome, half his sperms are lacking this sex-related chromosome. An egg fertilized by an X-carrying sperm develops into a girl, with two X chromosomes. If one of her X chromosomes carries a gene responsible for the type of congenital deafness just mentioned, the normal partner gene (allele) in her other X chromosome suffices to secure normal hearing. This situation obtains in sex-linked recessive inheritance. The man who delivers the X chromosome with the deafness gene is deaf, he lacks a normal partner gene as he carries only one X chromosome. He is unable to hand down the deaf-

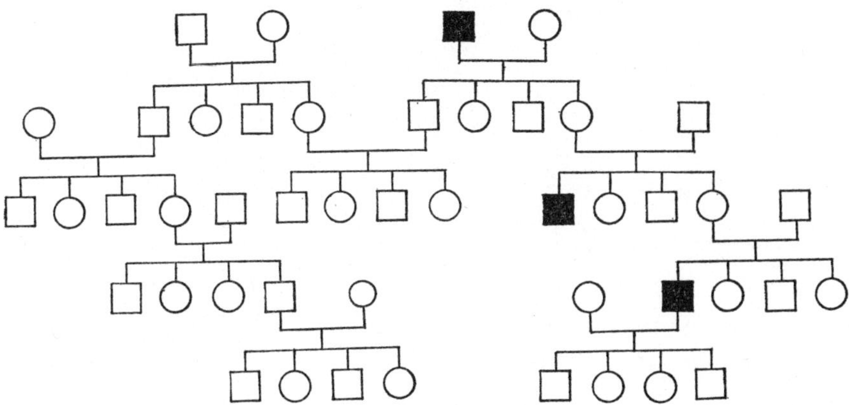

Figure VI-3. Sex-linked recessive inheritance. Model pedigree. Symbols as in Figure VI-1.

ness gene to his sons, his daughters will all carry the damaging gene. A carrier woman propagates this gene to 50 per cent of her daughters, who become carriers with normal hearing, and to 50 per cent of her sons, who become deaf.

It has been estimated that about 6 per cent of male cases of congenital deafness is accounted for by sex-linked recessive inheritance. A conductive type of deafness with stapes fixation and another type, with some hearing in early childhood and progredient severe hearing loss, neural, also conform to this mode of inheritance.

FAMILIAL BUT NOT HERITABLE

Some pedigree charts with deafness remain inexplicable and scarcity of data are not always the main difficulty. Deaf people tend to found families within their set, deafness by various external causes is not heritable but may convey a confusing impression when reported as hearing impairment among several ancestors. A special instance, where genes are in fact at play, concerns deafness caused by blood group incompatibility between mother and fetus. Some husband-wife combinations, often within the Rh system, expose fetuses to attack against their red blood cells by antibodies developed by their mothers. Several sibs can be affected and hearing impairment due to damage of auditory nuclei may be a prominent feature. Such deafness is not transmitted to subsequent generations.

Nor is fetal damage with hearing loss produced by drugs or pesticides inheritable. There is some reason to keep this seemingly self evident fact in mind as chemical agents capable of producing defects in the embryo are also known or suspected mutagens. We know through observational evidence in man and experiments in other organisms that detrimental genes now and then arise through new mutations. It is rarely possible to point, with some confidence, the deafness as arising by mutation in a given family, alternative explanations usually prevail. But mutant genes are transmitted and those of hearing impairment provide no exceptions. Mothers of deaf and malformed children are increasingly aware of ionizing radiation and chemical mutagens as possible causes of damage. Keeping apart mutation, arising in the sex cells of a normal man or woman, and fetal damage through exposure in early pregnancy, we can assert that the former is propagated to new generations, the latter is not.

DEVIANT PATTERNS OF INHERITANCE

For a variety of reasons simple patterns of inheritance often seem to be more or less obscured when hearing impairment is concerned. Still the basic idea of a specific disorder caused by a specific gene is of practical as well as theoretical use. The mutant gene can be autosomal or X-borne, inheritance can be dominant or recessive, but the most common basic risk figures, 50 and 25 per cent, may often represent limiting values.

When a deaf parent has more than the expected 50 per cent deaf children, in the case of autosomal dominant inheritance, chance is usually at play. It is no proof of especially *strong inheritance,* as the detrimental gene can just be present or absent. Now and then it so happens that the chromosome carrying the mutant gene again and again partakes in the formation of a new individual. It may be added that families with affected children being over represented tend to be fairly common in published reports.

Deaf family members below expected proportions are representative of chance deviations, but also of forces tending to reduce the manifestation rate of the detrimental gene. Variable age of onset can be looked upon as one step in the direction of reduced manifestation rate. In dominant midfrequency hearing loss the expected 1:1 proportions are valid for children well above ten years of age, in younger children of affected persons the hearing impairment may be overlooked or non-existent. Impaired hearing due to otosclerosis is observed in a few carriers of the detrimental gene as early as the first decade of life, but usually in the third decade. In rare instances the onset is as late as after fifty. Otosclerosis is dominantly inherited, but normally hearing gene carriers are fairly common. Even when attaining the age of onset, less than 50 per cent of men and women carrying the gene for otosclerosis become manifestly hard of hearing. Reduced penetrance, as such decreased manifestation rate is termed, comes to the foremost conspicuously in dominant inheritance, where some affected persons, against basic rules, are observed to have normal parents. In the case of otosclerosis an affected person can be told that the risk of a particular child being hard of hearing is less than 50 per cent, and probably less than 25 per cent. On the other hand a normally hearing brother or sister of a patient with otosclerosis can not be given the usual assurance of freedom from the detrimental gene valid for normal sibs in regularly dominant inheritance.

Whenever possible, penetrance figures should be calculated from observed manifestation rates in the actual family group as penetrance may vary from one kindred to another. When, for instance, four of ten sibships with an affected member lack an affected parent, penetrance amounts to 60 per cent. Though useful to denote such numerical facts the term penetrance imparts no explanation of the success or failure of a gene to become manifest. Factors more or less clearly related to penetrance are age, sex (in otosclerosis a higher manifestation rate in females than in males), environmental influences and genes other than the *main* gene. Similar modifying elements seem to be at play in irregularities of gene manifestation observed in various forms of deafness complicated with anomalies of organs and tissues unrelated to the organ of hearing. In osteogenesis imperfecta the mutant gene signals its presence in about nine carriers of ten by a bluish tinge to their scleras (outer envelopes of eyeballs). Most carriers of this gene have abnormally brittle bones and some of them become deaf. Blue scleras, brittleness of bones and deafness occur as alternative gene manifestations in different persons, a situation termed variable expressivity. Two or three manifestations also occur combined in the same gene carrier.

In some instances alternative gene expressions may be of help in tracing carriers of deafness genes and clarifying modes of inheritance. Blue scleras serve both purposes, another instance is ear pits in family members of persons with a special type of deafness. A fairly uncommon, if not rare, small pit at the front of the ear can be seen in families free from deafness, the inconspicuous trait is dominantly inherited, with reduced penetrance. In exceptional instances deteriorating hearing and ear pits may, however, be manifestations of the same mutant gene.

Today knowledge about the erratic ways of gene action in the field of human hearing impairment is incomplete. From a practical point of view it is important to remember that the sum of genes, rare and fairly common, capable of impairing the hearing function and inconspicuous in most carriers, is far from small. Freak pedigree charts with two deaf parents, expected to have only deaf children but raising large hearing broods, can sometimes be explained by the parental deafness being caused by different mutant genes.

As for pedigree charts, they serve a useful purpose when family data are summarized and interpreted. Published pedigrees often exclude negative information so that, for instance, normal mates are left out in charting dominant inheritance. Sibships are conventionally marked by coupling bars above the individual signs for brothers and sisters, mating bars are drawn between or beneath husband and wife. Squares are used for males, circles for females, affected persons are marked with filled symbols, unaffected with unfilled. Special signs are used quite liberally to embrace a variety of information, such as skin and skeletal anomalies in families with impaired hearing.

SYNDROMES

A formidable host of anomalies has been described as associated with deafness. Among those of skin pigmentation combined with hearing impairment, partial albinism in persons with profound childhood deafness may represent a mode of inheritance not mentioned thus far. Affected men have deaf and pigment-poor daughters and normal sons, affected women have normal and affected sons and daughters in equal proportions. This mode of transmission, sex-linked dominant, is rare in conditions with impaired hearing and by and large in human inheritance as known today.

Sex-linked recessive inheritance has been observed in several families with congenital and severe neural deafness associated with piebaldness (spotted pigmentary changes). Other X-borne genes give rise to one type of gargoylism, i.e. dwarfism with mental retardation and deposits of a mucopolysaccharide in various organs (Hunter's syndrome) and for dwarfism combined with cleft palate and generalized bone changes (oto-palato-digital or OPD syndrome), both these syndromes include congenital deafness. It is important to distinguish X-borne syndromes from superficially similar disorders caused by autosomal genes as female carriers have different family prospects in the two instances.

Among syndromes with deafness and autosomal dominant inheritance nephropathy is worth mentioning. In Alport's syndrome, as this disease is called, high tone sensorineural hearing loss occurs in some patients. It can be insignificant and demonstrable only by audiometry. Another dominantly transmitted syndrome, Waardenburg's, combines mild or severe congenital hearing loss with flat and broad nasal root and confluent eyebrows, plus more or less inconstant traits such as white forelock, one brown and one blue iris, spotty de- and hyperpigmentation of the skin and cleft lip or palate. Numerous autosomal dominant syndromes with deafness and skin anomalies have been reported, among them the leopard syndrome: widespread freckles growing in size and number, heart abnormalities, stunted growth and underdeveloped sex organs.

To recessive syndromes with deafness belongs hereditary goiter combined with congenital neural hearing loss (Pendred's syndrome). Pigmentary changes in the eye fundus in congenitally deaf children (Usher's syndrome) are associated with decreasing vision and blindness in teenagers or young adults. A third recessive syndrome includes mental deterioration, progressive ataxia (loss of muscular coordination) and hormonal changes in association with severe and early decrement of hearing.

For practical family planning it is necessary to take heed of any anomaly associated with hearing impairment, and to be most wary of the diagnoses they may suggest. There is a considerable overlapping between manifestations of different syndromes and irregularities in the appearance of particular signs, including deafness, are common. It will often be necessary to turn to special literature and consult specialists in different fields of medicine before a rare syndrome can be identified. On the other hand syndromes with impaired hearing constitute a substantial part of congenital deafness and call for help and advice to afflicted families in several respects.

COUNSELING AND DIRECTIVE GUIDANCE

The genetic counselor can aid family planning by presenting risk figures as accurately as humanly possible. He can also explain what is meant by his figures and how chance may strike. Then prospective parents can form their own decisions.

Other advisers with professional contact with deaf people and their families may find that their responsibility does not end there. Highly gifted people may hesitate to marry and found families because of a trifling risk of having hard of hearing children. Should they be encouraged to become parents or examined with regard to neurotic traits behind their hesitancy? Parents with health problems may be in doubt whether they are able to endure the burden of a severely handicapped child. To some women pregnancy with such expectations may become a too heavy burden. When explicitly asked for directive guidance physicians and family advisers can take into account risks that are not entirely connected with the laws of inheritance. Then it may be well to remember that deaf people do not come from tainted stock. We all carry detrimental genes. Impaired hearing without additional infirmity is a bearable burden. If we make gifted and responsible people abstain from having families we may deprive society of needed members and individuals of a source of happiness we cannot make up for.

REFERENCES

Bergstrom, LaVonne; Hemenway, W. G., and Downs, M.: A high risk registry to find congenital deafness. *Otolaryngologic Clinics of N Am, 4*:369, 1971.

Chazan, J. A.; Zacks, Jessica; Cohen, J. J., and Garella, S.: Hereditary nephritis: Clinical spectrum and mode of inheritance in five kindreds. *Am J Med, 50*:764, 1971.

Dolowitz, D. A.: An appraisal of genetics in clinical otology. *Ann Otol, 80*:264, 1971.

Fraser, G. R.: Sex-linked recessive congenital deafness and the excess of males in profound childhood deafness. *Ann Hum Genet, Lond, 29*:171, 1965.

Gacek, R.: The pathology of hereditary sensorineural hearing loss. *Ann Otol, 80*:289, 1971.

Konigsmark, B. W.: Hereditary deafness with external ear abnormalities. *The Johns Hopkins Med J, 127*:228, 1970.

Konigsmark, B. W.; Salman, Salah; Haskins, Harriet, and Mengel, M.: Dominant midfrequency hearing loss. *Ann Otol, 79:*42, 1970.

Konigsmark, B. W.: Hereditary congenital severe deafness syndromes. *Ann Otol, 80:*269, 1971.

Konigsmark, B. W.: Hereditary childhood hearing loss and integumentary system disease. *J Pediat, 80:*909, 1972.

McKusick, V. A.: *Mendelian Inheritance in Man,* 3rd ed. Baltimore, The Johns Hopkins Press, 1971.

McLeod, A. C.; McConnell, F. E.; Sweeney, Anne; Cooper, M. Claire and Nance, W. E.: Clinical variation in Usher's syndrome. *Arch Otolaryng, 94:*321, 1971.

Nance, W. E.: The principles and practice of genetic counseling. *Ann Otol, 80:*246, 1971.

Pashyan, H.; Fraser, F. C., and Goldbloom, R. B.: A family showing hereditary nephropathy. *Amer J Hum Genet, 23:*555, 1971.

Pickering, D.; Laski, B.; MacMillan, D. C., and Rose, Vera: *Little Leopard* syndrome. *Arch Dis Childhood, 46:*85, 1971.

Ruben, R. J. and Rozycki, D. L.: Clinical aspects of genetic deafness. *Ann Otol, 80:*255, 1971.

Sullivan, J. H.: Severe hearing defects in the pre-school child. *J Irish Med Assn, 64:*76, 1971.

Telfer, M. A.; Sugar, M.; Jaeger, E. A., and Mulcahy, J.: Dominant piebald trait (white forelock and leukoderma) with neurological impairment. *Amer J Hum Genet, 23:*383, 1971.

Turner, J. S.: Hereditary hearing loss with nephropathy (Alport's syndrome). *Acta oto-laryng,* Suppl *271,* 26 pp, 1970.

Chapter VII

THE DEAF STUDENT IN COLLEGES AND UNIVERSITIES

STEPHEN P. QUIGLEY

IN THE SEPTEMBER, 1962 issue of the *American Annals of the Deaf,* Schein and Bushnaq presented data comparing the growth in enrollment of hearing and deaf students in higher education between the years 1900 and 1960. The data indicated clearly the dramatic increase in enrollment of hearing students in institutions of higher education and the almost complete lack of proportionate increase for deaf students over the sixty year period. The data are presented in terms of the total college enrollment for each group as compared to the respective total school enrollment below college. On this basis the ratio of college students, both hearing and deaf, to their respective elementary and secondary populations in 1900 was approximately 1 to 100. By 1960 this ratio had risen to 9 per 100 for the hearing population, but only to 1.5 per 100 for deaf students. While the Schein and Bushnaq data for deaf students involved primarily Gallaudet College enrollment, estimates of the numbers of deaf students in other institutions of higher education did not raise the ratio appreciably.

There has been remarkable growth in programs in higher education for deaf students in the ten years since the Schein and Bushnaq article appeared. At the time they wrote, Gallaudet College was the only institution of higher education devoted to deaf students. Such is no longer the case. The program at Gallaudet College itself has been greatly expanded; the National Technical Institute for the Deaf has been established on the campus of the Rochester Institute of Technology in Rochester, New York; two federal agencies, the Bureau of Education for the Handicapped and the Social and Rehabilitation Service, have provided support for special programs for deaf students at Delgado College in New Orleans, Louisiana, Seattle Community College in Seattle, Washington, and St. Paul Technical and Vocational Institute in St. Paul, Minnesota; about twenty other institutions of higher education have established programs for deaf students without special federal funds; and substantial numbers of deaf students also are attending colleges and universities without any special programs for them. While data comparable to those of Schein and Bushnaq are not available for the present time, it seems likely that college enrollment for deaf students has proportionately outpaced that for hearing students during the past decade. There has been approximately a 50 per cent increase in the hearing college population from about 9,500,000 in 1960 to about 14,500,000 in 1970 (Froelich and Carey, 1969). It is likely that the college population of deaf students in all types of institutions of higher education quadrupled or more during the same period.

Much of the rapid increase in higher education opportunities for deaf students was due to the efforts of interested individuals and organizations; much, however, was due also to the Zeitgeist —the spirit of the times. Two factors in particular were involved: the tremendous growth in general college and university enrollment during the 1960's, and the clamor of minority groups for open admissions of some type in institutions of higher education. Rapid expansion of enrollment resulted partly from children from the post World War II *baby boom* reaching college age and partly from the impetus supplied by federal funds flowing freely into higher education following the Soviet Union's launching of Sputnik I. Just as the establishment of Gallaudet College in 1864 during the Lincoln era was related to the interest in general development of colleges and universities through the Land Grant Act of 1862, so the rapid development of facilities and programs for the higher education of deaf students during the decade of the 1960's was related to the developments in general higher education just described. Massive involvement of public funds in programs for handicapped individuals, including those who are deaf, takes place along with or following similar involvement with education in general. It does not precede the general development.

The demands for less restrictive admission requirements at colleges and universities followed from the demands by minority groups for economic and social justice including equal access to educational opportunities at all levels. The resulting pressure on institutions of higher education produced increased resources and programs for students who formerly had no chance of being admitted to most colleges and universities. Admission requirements were lowered, or manipulated in other ways, and special programs of tutoring and other services were provided for the students who needed them. While the initial demands for social justice and equal educational opportunities came mostly from black people, the benefits of changed admission policies and other attitudes on the part of university administrations were felt also by other minority groups, including deaf people.

Besides paralleling and following the great expansion of higher education in general, postsecondary programs for deaf students have tended to reflect the trends of development in educational programs for deaf students below the college level. Thus the diversity of educational programs for deaf students in residential schools, day schools, day classes, and regular public and private school classes have their respective counterparts in Gallaudet College (residential school), the National Technical Institute for the Deaf (day school), the special programs in junior and community colleges (day class), and attendance in any institution of higher education with little or no special help (regular public and private school classes). This parallel in development between postsecondary programs for deaf students and those at the elementary and secondary level did not result from deliberate planning with the various postsecondary programs being established as more advanced counterparts of the different types of programs at the lower levels. Rather, they likely resulted from the conscious or unconscious application of the philosophy of separating education of deaf persons, as of any minority group, as little as possible from the general public school programs. Completely segregated programs of education for minority groups rarely remain equal to programs for the general populace, except over relatively short periods of time when the public conscience is uneasy for some reason.

It is important that the development of higher education programs for deaf students has produced choices for them in the extent to which they can segregate or interact with the general student population in higher education. Perhaps more important, however, is the increased range of educational choices made available to them in terms of specific training programs. Gallaudet College and the National Technical Institute for the Deaf provide the foundation of higher education for deaf students. Between them they offer a wide range of liberal arts and technical programs which will continue to be needed by deaf students for probably as long as deafness is with us. However, as Quigley, Jenné, and Phillips (1968) emphasized in a study of deaf students in general institutions of higher education, a system of specialized facilities and programs for a small population can never duplicate the vast array of educational opportunities available to the general population. Until deafness is eliminated, it would seem advisable to invest some resources in determining how existing educational facilities and programs can be made more readily available to those who are deaf. This is being done in some of the programs which have been mentioned and which will be discussed in more detail. While the formidable barriers to the entrance of deaf students into general institutions of higher education presented by their language, communication, and educational problems should not be underestimated, neither should they be overestimated. Present programs in higher education for other minority groups indicate that past admission requirements have often been unnecessarily restrictive. Also, the opening of doors for deaf students into colleges and universities will likely raise the aspiration levels of deaf students, their parents, and their schools. This, along with the developments in their precollege programs such as early childhood education, early language development, and comprehensive secondary schools, will likely increase their educational and language levels in future years and make them more competitive with the general college population.

Some of the recently established programs in higher education for deaf students, such as the National Technical Institute for the Deaf, were the result of considerable planning; others, such as the special programs in a number of junior and community colleges, were probably preceded by little planning. Certainly, the system of programs now existing at the postsecondary level, while it is a rather logical one, was not developed as a system, but grew piece by piece. Perhaps this is a good time to look at the pieces to see how they fit together into a system, what pieces might still be missing, and what directions future developments might most profitably take. The term *postsecondary* is being used interchangeably with *higher education* to denote any educational program beyond the secondary school level.

Postsecondary Programs for Deaf Students

The reader will find two references of primary importance in locating the various postsecondary programs now available to deaf students. In the July, 1969 issue of the *Journal of Rehabilitation of the Deaf* is a series of papers delivered at the 1969 convention of the Professional Rehabilitation Workers with the Adult Deaf. Articles describe programs at Gallaudet College, the National Technical Institute for the Deaf, Delgado College in New Orleans, Seattle Community College, St. Paul Technical and Vocational Institute, and a study by Quigley, Jenné, and Phillips (1968) of several hundred deaf students who attended several hundred institutions of higher education which made no special provisions for deaf students. (Other articles in the issue describe various community programs of rehabilitation and psychiatric services for deaf people, and the entire issue is worthy of study.) The second reference is an article by Stuckless (1972) which lists twenty-two operational postsecondary programs for deaf students distributed throughout fourteen states and the District of Columbia and four additional programs expected to

TABLE VII-I

INSTRUCTIONAL EMPHASIS, CERTIFICATES AWARDED, AND NUMBER OF FULL-TIME DEAF STUDENTS IN EACH OF 22 OPERATIONAL PROGRAMS

	Instructional Emphasis		*Certificates of Degrees Awarded*				
			Cert./Assoc.				
Institution	*Arts & Sciences*	*Tech./Voc.*	*Diploma*	*Degree*	*Baccalaureate Degree*	*Graduate Degree*	*No Full-time Deaf Students, Fall, 1971*
1.	x	x	x	x			70
2.		x	x				77
3.	x	x	x	x			27
4.	x	x	x	x			*
5.	x				x	x	52
6.		x	x	x			86
7.	x				x	x	1009
8.	x	x		x			20
9.	9 month preparatory and exploratory program		x				32
10.	x	x	x	x			12
11.	x	x	x	x			14
12.		x	x				18
13.		x	x	x			75
14.	x	x	x	x			*
15.		x	x				18
16.		x	x				90
17.		x	x	x	x	x	338
18.	preparation for the ministry		x				7
19.	x	x	x	x			7
20.		x	x	x			50
21.		x	x	x			*
22.	x	x	x	x			92
TOTALS .	11	18	19	14	3	3	2094

* Became operational since Fall term.

Note.—Reprinted from an article by E. Ross Stuckless published in the June 1972 *American Annals of the Deaf*.

open in September, 1973. Stuckless estimates that these twenty-two programs, which include Gallaudet College and the National Technical Institute for the Deaf, enroll about 2100 students. If we add to this number the two hundred or more deaf students who probably are enrolled in other institutions of higher education in any given year, the resulting total provides substantiation for the earlier statement that enrollment of deaf students in higher education probably has at least quadrupled since the Schein and Bushnaq (1962) study. The two references just discussed are valuable sources of information for parents, and for counselors, teachers, and administrators at the lower school level. The article by Stuckless contains the name and address of a person in each program who can be contacted for information concerning the program.

TABLE VII-II

INDICATION OF SOME OF THE SPECIAL SERVICES OFFERED DEAF STUDENTS BY EACH OF THE 22 OPERATIONAL PROGRAMS

Institution	*Preparatory Activities*	*Interpreting*	*Tutoring*	*Notetaking*	*Vocational Counseling*	*Personal and Social Counseling*	*Vocational Placement*	*Speech and/or Hearing Services*	*Academic Advising*	*Manual Comm. Training*	*Supervised Housing*
1.	x	x		x				x		x	
2.	x	x	x	x	x	x	x	x	x	x	x
3.		x	x	x	x	x			x	x	
4.	x	x	x	x	x	x	x	x	x	x	
5.	x	x	x	x	x	x	x	x	x	x	
6.	x	x	x	x	x	x	x		x	x	
7.	x		x		x	x	x	x	x	x	x
8.	x	x	x	x	x	x	x		x	x	
9.	x	x	x	x	x	x	x	x	x	x	x
10.	x	x	x	x	x	x	x		x	x	
11.	x	x	x	x	x	x	x	x	x	x	
12.	x	x	x		x	x	x	x	x	x	
13.	x	x	x	x	x	x			x	x	
14.	x	x	x	x		x			x	x	
15.	x	x	x	x	x	x	x	x	x	x	x
16.	x	x	x	x	x	x	x	x	x	x	x
17.	x	x	x	x	x	x	x	x	x	x	x
18.		x				x			x		x
19.	x	x	x	x	x	x	x	x	x	x	
20.	x	x	x	x	x	x	x		x	x	x
21.		x	x	x	x		x		x		
22.	x	x	x	x	x	x	x	x	x	x	x
TOTALS	19	21	20	19	19	20	17	13	21	20	9

Note.—Reprinted from an article by E. Ross Stuckless published in the June 1972 *American Annals of the Deaf*.

Gallaudet College

Higher education for deaf persons has been provided traditionally by Gallaudet College, a privately incorporated institution in the liberal arts and sciences located in Washington, D. C. The College was established in 1864 through the efforts of Edward Miner Gallaudet and is named in honor of his father, Thomas Hopkins Gallaudet, who founded in Hartford, Connecticut, in 1817 the first permanent school in the United States for deaf individuals. It is largely supported in its capital and operating budgets, directly and indirectly, by the Federal Government. Until about 1950, the College was regarded largely as an institution for the preparation of deaf teachers. Since that time its curriculum has been expanded to a comprehensive program in the liberal arts and sciences, its faculty has been increased and diversified, most of the campus has been rebuilt, the College has become an accredited institution, and the student body has increased from little more than two hundred to slightly more than one thousand. In addition to providing for deaf students a four year program in liberal arts and sciences, the College has graduate programs for preparing teachers and other specialists to work with deaf persons and a one year preparatory program. Due to inadequate educational and language development, approximately 80 per cent of the entering students must complete the preparatory year to gain admission to the college program.

In 1966 the Model Secondary School for the Deaf was established by Public Law 89-694 on the campus of Gallaudet College, and Public Law 91-587 in 1970 transformed the Kendall School for the Deaf (which is located on the campus of Gallaudet College) into a federally financed model program at the elementary school level. As Greenberg (1969) has pointed out:

> With the Model Secondary School, Gallaudet will have on its grounds the entire spectrum of deaf education. It is intriguing to consider that a deaf student might enter our pre-school program, continue on through Kendall and the Model Secondary School, get both bachelor's and master's degrees and end up as a faculty member—all without having left the campus. While no one would sug-

gest such an encapsulated educational career would be desirable, it remains technically feasible.

In the parallel drawn earlier between the developing system of higher education programs for deaf students and the system of precollege educational programs, Gallaudet College was seen as functioning similarly to the residential school portion of the lower school system. This simply means that its educational programs are mostly contained and operated within its own campus and that most of its students live on the campus. The educational and social environment is therefore similar to that of a residential school in that the students are relatively isolated from the larger community. In the past this represented a continuation of the environment to which most of the College's students had earlier been exposed, since most of them came from residential schools. As Greenberg (1969) has indicated, however, more than 25 per cent of students in the College now come from public high schools, preparatory schools, and colleges as compared to only four or five per cent in 1950. Besides diversifying the sources from which it draws its student body, Gallaudet has taken many other steps to involve its students with the general community and increasing interaction is planned between the student body and the student bodies of other colleges and universities. Nevertheless, Gallaudet remains essentially similar to the residential school in the segregation of its student body from the general population. In this it is quite different from the other major specialized institution of higher education for deaf students—the National Technical Institute for the Deaf.

The National Technical Institute for the Deaf

The National Technical Institute for the Deaf was created in 1965 by Public Law 89-36 to provide postsecondary technical education for deaf persons. Open competition for the facility among institutions of higher education resulted in its being awarded to the Rochester Institute of Technology in Rochester, New York, in 1966. Ground was broken for construction of NTID facilities on the campus of RIT in 1971 and completion of construction is expected by 1974. Completion of facilities will enable the NTID to reach its planned enrollment of 750 deaf students. Instruction began with a pilot group of seventy students in 1968 and presently about five hundred students are being served.

Students pursue preparatory courses (as in Gallaudet College) and can enter certificate, diploma, or degree programs which suit their interests and abilities. The broad spectrum of programs includes such career areas as technical science, visual communication, social sciences, and business and engineering technologies which can lead to technical, semiprofessional, and professional careers in business, industry, government, and education (Frisina, 1969). In one sense, the National Technical Institute for the Deaf is a technical counterpart of Gallaudet College. Together they offer to deaf students a wide range of educational opportunities in liberal arts, sciences, and technical subjects; in combination they are a university in miniature.

Gallaudet College and the National Technical Institute for the Deaf differ in the types of educational programs they offer to deaf students. They differ also in the extent to which their programs interact with those of other institutions of higher education. The programs of Gallaudet College are largely self-contained, those of the NTID are not. When the NTID was planned, it was with the express philosophy that it should be a part of an existing institution of higher education upon whose resources it could draw. The NTID was to supply those support services and special programs which deaf students could not readily pursue or hope to succeed with in the parent institution, and the students would have available to them the wide array of programs of the parent institution. The NTID has actively pursued that philosophy from its establishment at RIT. Students can enroll in the programs of the RIT, for one class or a total program, and receive whatever assistance they need from the special NTID staff and resources to help them succeed. At the same time, the philosophy of the NTID recognizes that many deaf students can be expected to succeed with only very little of the regular RIT offerings and must have programs designed exclusively for them and taught by special instructors as at Gallaudet. Thus, the deaf student has a whole range of programs from those completely contained within the NTID to those completely contained with the RIT. Most students have programs along the continuum between the two extremes.

As mentioned earlier, a system of specialized facilities and programs for a small population, such as the deaf population, can never equal the vast array of educational opportunities available to the general population. Some means must be found to make existing educational programs and facilities available to those who are deaf. The NTID is one way in which the vast resources of institutions of higher education can be opened to deaf students. It represents a giant step forward in higher education for deaf people. From one point of view the NTID is similar to the day school programs which provide special educational programs for deaf students within the public school system, but attempt to integrate the students with hearing students in regular programs. The analogy here, however, is less clear cut than in the case of Gallaudet College and the residential school. The close cooperation between the NTID and the RIT and the active planning for integration of deaf students that has taken place, seems to have produced a much greater interaction of the deaf and hearing student bodies than occurs in day school or even in day class programs. More similar in philosophy to the day class programs, perhaps, are the regional programs for deaf students which have been established with federal support at Delgado College, Seattle Community College, and the St. Paul Technical and Vocational Institute.

Regional Postsecondary Programs

A federally supported project was initiated in 1968 to 1969 to increase the vocational and technical opportunities for deaf students by establishing pilot postsecondary programs in three schools in different sections of the country: Delgado College in New Orleans, Louisiana (Wells, 1969); Seattle Community College in Seattle, Washington (Brookey, 1969); and St. Paul Technical and Vocational Institute in St. Paul, Minnesota (Nelson, 1969). The basic aim was to utilize programs already available for hearing students by carefully and systematically integrating deaf students into the programs in accordance with their abilities and interests. Supportive services were supplied specifically for deaf students to enable them to compete successfully in the regular programs. These services consisted mostly of classes in language and communication, tutoring in subjects with which a student had difficulty, and specialized counseling. A guiding philosophy of the programs was that they would not supply as a special service for deaf students any service which was available through the regular school staff.

In addition to supporting financially the three postsecondary programs, the Bureau of Education for the Handicapped and the Social and Rehabilitation Service established a unit to coordinate the programs and to conduct a continuing evaluation of their effectiveness. Craig (1970) described this unit, the three postsecondary programs, and the relations between the research unit and the programs. Craig's article indicated that each of the three programs had a projected enrollment of one hundred deaf students while in 1970 actual enrollment was sixty-one at Delgado, forty-two at Seattle Community College, and forty-nine at St. Paul Technical and Vocational Institute. The article also listed the career objectives most frequently selected by students in the three programs as being graphic arts, prosthetics, production art, college parallel, electronics, sheet metal, welding, auto body, food services, and machine tool processing.

The regional postsecondary programs may be considered as analogous to the day class programs for deaf students at the elementary and secondary school level. The philosophy is to keep the deaf student in the mainstream of the general educational process as much as possible, and to supply for him only those special services which he needs because of his deafness. This means primarily the supplying of specially trained personnel rather than special programs or facilities. The postsecondary programs have avoided one of the major problems of day classes —the establishment of programs with too few students to make providing the necessary special personnel economically practical. If the programs prove to be successful, they could represent a significant breakthrough in postsecondary education for deaf students, since the guidelines resulting from the research unit's evaluation should enable similar programs to be established in many of the junior and community colleges which have become the most rapidly expanding part of the higher education system in the United States. A number of such programs, in fact, have already been established.

Local Postsecondary Programs

The designation of programs as *local* is used simply to differentiate them from the programs just described which were established as regional programs with the express purpose of drawing students from a defined number of states. As pointed out by Stuckless (1972), the mushrooming of local postsecondary institutions has resulted in the emergence of about 1,100 community colleges with an enrollment of almost 3,000,000 students. These institutions offer distinct opportunities for deaf students, since their admission requirements are much less restrictive than those of the typical four year institution, many of their programs are vocationally oriented and suitable for deaf students, and they have as a priority relevance to the needs of the communities in which they are located.

Stuckless (1972) has listed twenty-two programs which already are operational and four more which are about to become operational. This list includes the programs at Gallaudet College, the National Technical Institute for the Deaf, Delgado College, Seattle Community College, and St. Paul Technical and Vocational Institute which have already been described. Thus, the list contains information of value to educators, rehabilitation counselors, parents, and deaf persons in making decisions about placement in higher education. Because of this importance, the list of institutions is reproduced, with the permission of its author, at the end of this chapter along with two tables from the same article which describe the instructional emphasis, certificates awarded, number of full time deaf students, and some of the special services offered deaf students in each of the twenty-two operational programs.

It will be obvious that these programs are even more similar to the day class programs of the lower school system than are the regional postsecondary programs. In addition to participating as much as possible in the regular educational programs of the institutions, most of the students are likely to live in or near their homes. The philosophy of supplying only those special services rendered necessary by deafness is similar in the postsecondary and lower school programs. Another group of deaf students can be found attending institutions of higher education which do not provide special programs, and these students can be considered analogous to those (probably few) students at the lower levels who somehow manage to attend successfully the regular public and private elementary and secondary school programs.

Deaf Students in Colleges and Universities

For many years the *Volta Review* has published annual listings of deaf persons known to be attending institutions of higher education, other than those with special programs for deaf students, and some descriptive information on those persons and the programs they attended. In 1968 Quigley, Jenné, and Phillips published the report of a more detailed study of this matter. Their study was conducted to determine the extent to which deaf persons were successful in attending regular colleges and universities in the United States and the characteristics which were associated with attendance of deaf students in such institutions. By a variety of techniques, 902 persons were located who seemed to meet the study criteria, and a total of 653 respondents returned questionnaires which were useable for the purposes of the study.

The study showed that considerable numbers of deaf persons seek higher education in regular colleges and universities. It also showed that many such persons graduate successfully from those institutions and attain professional status in the occupational world commensurate with their educational attainments. Since the success of these individuals is achieved with little or no special assistance, it would seem reasonable to assume that the provision of special services, such as are available to blind and other handicapped students, would make it possible for greater numbers of deaf persons to achieve similar success in regular colleges and universities. A number of recommendations concerning this matter were presented in the report.

1. Special counseling should be provided early in the second-

ary school years for students who seem to have the academic and intellectual potential for higher education. The student should be made familiar with the wide range of universities, colleges, community colleges, and specialized institutes which are available. He should be given the information necessary for making the most appropriate choice in terms of his interests and abilities. Assistance should be provided to aid him in gaining admission to an appropriate institution.

2. Special counseling and special services should be made available to the student when he enters an institution of higher education. Respondents in the study indicated a need for assistance in both academic and social areas in such matters as admission procedures, orientation to the institution, special and career counseling and guidance.

Provision of special services to increase the chances of success for more deaf students in regular institutions of higher education would undoubtedly be expensive, since they would require a very low ratio of clients per counselor and other special personnel. Such services, however, would be much less expensive than the provision of specialized facilities. In addition to the lower expense of such a program, it is obvious that the vast array of higher education programs available to the general population can never be duplicated by special facilities for a small population. Such special facilities are needed, but the deaf person will continue to be confronted with a restricted range of educational choices and opportunities until ways are found to make available to him the facilities and programs available to the general population.

The Future in Higher Education for Deaf Persons

Surprising as it might seem, it is difficult to find any significant pieces missing in the system of higher education opportunities for deaf people. As stated previously, the system was not developed as a system but grew piece by piece without any planned coordination among the pieces. Yet what has resulted is a rather comprehensive variety of programs. Prior to 1966 the deaf student interested in higher education had a choice, with a few exceptions, between Gallaudet College and attendance without special help in some other college or university. In rapid succession, we have had the establishment of the National Technical Institute for the Deaf, the three regional postsecondary programs, and the spontaneously generated local programs in many states. So the deaf student now has something approaching the diversity of educational opportunities available to the general population.

One major gap which might seem apparent is lack of continuing education opportunities for deaf people at the college level. But, this deficiency too has been remedied in recent months by the establishment at Gallaudet College of a federally funded program to stimulate continuing education for deaf people on a nationwide basis. The National Technical Institute for the Deaf has also been reaching outside its confines to stimulate improved programs of secondary and postsecondary education for deaf students. These efforts by the two national institutions to provide service for a wider constituency than just their own students are commendable and forward looking, provided they result in independent development of programs and facilities at the local and state levels rather than a collection of centrally controlled satellites.

While most of the pieces for a comprehensive system of higher education for deaf students now exists, some of the pieces are not yet solidly established. This is particularly true of the three regional postsecondary programs. Gallaudet College and the National Technical Institute for the Deaf are funded on a permanent basis primarily by the federal government, and it is unlikely that either institution could exist without that support. The regional centers are funded partly by local and state funds, but partly also by annual grants from the two sponsoring federal agencies. There is a great need to place this federal support on a permanent basis, or to determine how local and state support can bear the whole burden. A similar situation might develop in the local community college programs, if sufficient special services for deaf students are to be provided in those programs. The local and regional programs represent a great step forward in higher education for deaf people. Through their ability to provide access for deaf students into the general higher education system, they provide them with a diversity of educational opportunities which was lacking prior to 1965. And diversity of educational programs, philosophies, and approaches has been a distinguishing strength of American education.

There is a need also to begin studying the higher education programs for deaf students as a system. Most states are beginning to do this with general higher education, rather than allowing the various components to grow in isolation. In order to study the system and make projections for the future, overall planning needs to be done by some group similar to the Boards of Higher Education which have been established in many states. And that group will need information input which presently does not exist about the present and projected numbers of actual and potential deaf college students and the types of programs they will need. The beginnings of demographic study of deaf students in the educational system have been established by Gallaudet College with the support of the Bureau of Education for the Handicapped. It should be possible for that study, or study by a similar unit, to provide the projections of college enrollment for deaf students as is done presently by most states and by the federal government for the general population. Rational planning can hardly take place without such information, and rational development of programs can hardly take place without an overall planning board. It is fair to summarize the future for the deaf student in higher education by saying rather tritely that it is bright, much brighter than it was a mere six or seven years ago. With rational planning of the various programs as a system, that bright future could become still brighter.

POSTSECONDARY PROGRAMS FOR DEAF STUDENTS IN 1972

(a) Operational

1. Golden West College
   15744 Golden West Street
   Huntington Beach, California 92647
   For admissions information contact:
   Daniel Clere, Guidance Specialist
   (same address)
   Tel. 714-847-4489

2. Hacienda La Puente Valley Vocational School
   15359 E. Proctor
   City of Industry, California 91744
   For admissions information contact:
   Jean Smith, Coordinator,
   Deaf Program
   (same address)
   Tel. 213-968-4638
3. Riverside City College
   4800 Magnolia Avenue
   Riverside, California 92506
   For admissions information contact:
   William May, Coordinator for the Deaf
   (same address)
   Tel. 714-684-3240
4. San Diego Community Colleges
   835 Twelfth Avenue
   San Diego, California 92101
   For admissions information contact:
   Beverly McKee
   Acting Administrative Assistant for Deaf Programs
   733 Eighth Avenue
   San Diego, California 92101
   Tel. 714-232-7497
5. San Fernando Valley State College
   Northridge, California 91324
   For admissions information contact:
   Dr. Thomas Mayes, Coordinator
   Services for the Deaf
   Room 220 Engineering Building
   (same address)
   Tel. 213-885-2614
6. Community College of Denver
   1001 East 62nd Avenue
   Denver, Colorado 80216
   For admissions information contact:
   Theodore Guttadore, Director

Center for the Hearing Impaired
(same address)
Tel. 303-287-3311

7. Gallaudet College
Florida Avenue at 7th Street, N.E.
Washington, D. C. 20002
For admissions information contact:
Bernard Greenberg
Director of Admissions and Records
(same address)
Tel. 202-386-6555
8. St. Petersburg Junior College
Clearwater Campus
2465 Drew Street
Clearwater, Florida 33515
For admissions information contact:
Thomas Howze, Coordinator
Program for the Deaf
(same address)
Tel. 813-544-2551
9. Northern Illinois University
DeKalb, Illinois 60115
For admission information contact:
Gary Austin, Director
Program for the Speech and Hearing Impaired
(same address)
Tel. 815-753-1481
10. Iowa Western Community College
2700 College Road
Council Bluffs, Iowa 51501
For admissions information contact:
Bruce Hicks, Coordinator
Deaf Program
(same address)
Tel. 712-328-3831
11. Johnson County Community College
57 and Merriam Drive

Shawnee Mission, Kansas 66202
For admissions information contact:
Darrell Matthews, Coordinator
Program for the Hearing Impaired
(same address)
Tel. 913-236-4500

12. Jefferson County Area Vocational School
3101 Bluebird Lane
Jeffersontown, Kentucky 40299
For admissions information contact:
Jesse Wright, Counselor
(same address)
Tel. 502-267-7431

13. Delgado Vocational Technical Junior College
615 City Park Avenue
New Orleans, Louisiana 70119
For admissions information contact:
Douglas Wells, Project Director
(same address)
Tel. 504-486-5403

14. Genesee Community College
1401 East Court Street
Flint, Michigan 48503
For admissions information contact:
Bert Poss, Director
Program for Hearing Impaired Students
(same address)
Tel. 313-238-1631

15. State Technical Institute and Rehabilitation Center
Alber Drive
Plainwell, Michigan 49080
For admissions information contact:
Fred Daniels, Assistant Principal
(same address)
Tel. 616-664-4461

16. St. Paul Technical Vocational Institute
235 Marshall Avenue
St. Paul, Minnesota 55102

For admissions information contact:
Roger Reddan, Project Counselor
(same address)
Tel. 612-227-9121

17. National Technical Institute for the Deaf
Rochester Institute of Technology
1 Lomb Memorial Drive
Rochester, New York 14623
For admissions information contact:
Joseph Dengler, Coordinator of Admissions
(same address)
Tel. 716-464-2197

18. Tennessee Temple Schools
Chattanooga, Tennessee 37404
For admissions information contact:
L. D. Lockery, Registrar
(same address)
Tel. 615-698-1535

19. Eastfield College
3737 Motley Drive
Mesquite, Texas 75149
For admissions information contact:
Wilbur Dennis, Registrar
(same address)
Tel. 214-746-3100

20. Lee College
Box 818
Baytown, Texas 77520
For admissions information contact:
Thomas McGee, Project Director
210 Graystone Building
1209 Decker Drive
Baytown, Texas 77520
Tel. 713-427-6531

21. Tarrant County Junior College
Northeast Campus
828 Harwood Road
Hurst, Texas 76053

For admissions information contact:
James Reed, Programs Coordinator
1400 Fort Worth National Bank
Fort Worth, Texas 76102
Tel. 817-336-7851

22. Seattle Community College
1625 Broadway
Seattle, Washington 98122
For admissions information contact:
Stanley Traxler, Director
Program for the Deaf
(same address)
Tel. 206-587-4183

(b) Projected for enrollment of deaf students in September, 1972

23. American River College
4700 College Oak Drive
Sacramento, California 95841
For admissions information contact:
Robert Allerton, Dean of Student Personnel Services
(same address)
Tel. 916-484-8261

24. Santa Ana College
17th and Bristol
Santa Ana, California 92706
For admissions information contact:
Dr. Leroy Gloria, Dean of Special Service
(same address)
Tel. 714-547-9561

25. Columbus Technical Institute
550 East Spring Street
Columbus, Ohio 43215
For admissions information contact:
Douglas Slasor, Coordinator, Deaf Program
(same address)
Tel. 614-221-6743

26. Community College of Philadelphia
    34 South 11th Street
    Philadelphia, Pennsylvania 19107
    For admissions information contact:
    Harry Serotkin, Assistant to the President
    (same address)
    Tel. 215-569-3680

Note: Reprinted from an article by E. Ross Stuckless published in the June 1972 *American Annals of the Deaf.*

REFERENCES

Brookey, J. M.: The Seattle Community College new program for deaf people. *J Rehabil Deaf, 3:*52-60, 1969.

Craig, W. N.; Craig, H. B., and Burrows, N. L.: A progress report—postsecondary opportunities for deaf students. *The Volta Rev, 72:*290-295, 1970.

Frisina, D. R.: NTID and higher education for deaf persons. *J Rehabil Deaf, 3:*28-33, 1969.

Froelich, G. J. and Carey, R. C.: *Higher Education Enrollments in Illinois 1960-2000.* Urbana, Illinois: University Bureau of Institutional Research, University of Illinois, Urbana, December, 1969, p. 4.

Greenberg, B. L.: Gallaudet College: trends for the future. *J Rehabil Deaf, 3:*21-27, 1969.

Nelson, G. W.: The St. Paul Technical Institute program for deaf students. *J Rehabil Deaf, 3:*61-68, 1969.

Quigley, S. P.: Higher education for deaf persons in regular institutions. *J Rehabil Deaf, 3:*34-43, 1969.

Quigley, S. P.; Jenné, W. C., and Phillips, S. B.: *Deaf Students in Colleges and Universities.* Washington, D. C., Alexander Graham Bell Association for the Deaf, 1968.

Schein, J. D. and Bushnaq, S. M.: Higher education for the deaf in the United States: a retrospective investigation. *Am Ann Deaf, 107:*417-420, 1962.

Stuckless, E. R.: Postsecondary programs for deaf students in 1972. *Am Ann Deaf, 117:*377-382, 1972.

Wells, D. O.: The Delgado College academic and vocational education program for the deaf. *J Rehabil Deaf, 3:*44-51, 1969.

Chapter VIII

WORK ADJUSTMENT FOR PEOPLE WHO ARE DEAF

Robert A. Lassiter

Background

People who are deaf and who are in need of work adjustment services in the rehabilitation process need to be viewed first as human beings who are more similar than different to those with normal hearing: "In no way does deafness alter the person's need for love, esteem, acceptance, productivity and independence. . . . We may speak of a *psychology of deafness* if we are referring to their special learning and adjustment needs, but if we are using the term to suggest that all deaf people learn according to unique processes, or have unique personalities, then its use is unjustified" (Patterson and Stewart, 1971).

Perhaps the greatest problem that deaf people face in the adjustment to work is the inability of the rehabilitation professional worker to be able to communicate effectively with the deaf client in his language. Once this communication barrier is removed, the rehabilitation worker is better able to understand the client's special needs as an individual (as distinguished from the *needs of the deaf*). He will be able to become more aware of and more sensitive to the problems the individual deaf person may have in regard to social and personal needs, his feelings of isolation which he may have experienced in his own family, his feelings about the counselor and the counseling process, his expectations of the work adjustment plan, and his feelings and thoughts about the *world of work.* And, the counselor or other rehabilitation person, after eliminating this communication obstacle, will be able to understand better the deaf person's thoughts about his vocational interests, his feelings of competence and incompetence in certain tasks—to see these things from the client's frame of reference.

Without this ability to communicate in the client's language, e.g., The American Sign Language, the rehabilitation counselor or work adjustment person will become involved with the client in a lengthy and extremely difficult process in order to establish a relationship which will reflect accurately and realistically the client's view of himself in relation to his adjustment to a satisfactory job (Many deaf people in professional positions in rehabilitation may say it will be an impossible and futile task!).

Boyce Williams, Director of the Office of Deafness and Communicative Disorders in the Rehabilitation Services Administration, indicates that there also may be a need for rehabilitation workers to recognize that many deaf people are without useful speech and language skills, despite years of training; they receive information through their eyes. They impart information by a combination of signs, gestures, speech, and writing, although the large majority prefer signs between themselves and hearing persons who are masters of the sign language. Mary Ann Locke of the National Association of the Deaf has stated that the association is attempting to solve this problem by suggesting the use of the American Sign Language (Ameslan) by rehabilitation workers since most adult deaf people use the signs in communicating with each other. In addition to Ameslan she underscored the importance of the use of facial expressions as used in mime (the technique of portraying a character, mood, idea of narration by gestures and bodily movements). These expressions and movements are as necessary in using sign language as tone, inflection of voice, and facial expression are important to the hearing person in communicating with another. Fant (1972), who has developed a system of teaching sign language, reminds us in his teaching manual that *all languages have dialects, and the local variation of the signs are "our dialects" in the language of the deaf; therefore, by all means, use your local signs.*

Before exploring the special problems of deaf people's adjustment to work, it is important to look at what Dr. McCay Vernon, a prominent psychologist for deaf people, calls the crises of the deaf. Relative to the vocational crisis, he lists the following trends in the nation that he states are being ignored by the professionals who work with deaf persons:

> "1. . . . the alarming increase in unemployment among deaf people; 2. another trend jeopardizing the deaf worker's chance is automation. Over eighty per cent of employed deaf persons are in semi-skilled or unskilled manual labor. Fifty per cent of these are in manufacturing. It is these two areas where automation is making its greatest inroads. 3. Linotyping, compositing and presswork—long the main fields of employment for skilled deaf craftsmen and many deaf college graduates—are today trades of rapidly diminishing demands. 4. Another problem is that in the world of work there is an overall shift to white collar jobs in industry . . . unless there is an upgrading in present educational results, there is obviously little hope for deaf people to cash in on the increase in white collar jobs." (McCay, 1971).

These trends indicate a greater need for the development of work adjustment programs for deaf people than ever before. Despite the large number of deaf people who experience serious maladaptive problems in adult life and the increasing number of deaf children who have multiple handicapping conditions including mental retardation, etc., all studies dealing with intelligence show that *deaf people have the same intelligence as the normally hearing–their work habits are good, and employers who have hired deaf workers, at times reluctantly, have generally been pleased. . . . The solution to the problem is seen in providing proper and realistic educational opportunities through combined manual-oral communication, which breaks barriers to learning and to understanding, and frees their normal intellectual capacity* (Mindel and Vernon, 1971). The answer also lies in the ability of the rehabilitation leadership throughout the nation to require rehabilitation counselors and work adjustment personnel to be aware of the special needs of deaf people and what some of these trends hold for them; also, professional people who are employed to help deaf people in their adjustment to work must become proficient in the language of the deaf. Yes, for purposes of adjustment to the world of work, a deaf person must learn to *get along* in the hearing world—but, in order for him to do this, the professional person must learn to *get along* in the world of deafness.

Work Adjustment—A General Review

The work adjustment process is neither a new term nor an entirely new program in the field of rehabilitation. However, this aspect of the rehabilitation process continues to be misunderstood by administrators, and misinterpreted by many practitioners. As Hoffman said in a recent paper, "Work Adjustment, a treatment process utilizing work or aspects of work to modify behavior, is also at times defined as an evaluative process. It is not an evaluative process but is, as the words indicate, an adjustment or treatment process" (Hoffman, 1972). It is important to recognize this difference, and to acknowledge that the goals of work adjustment differ from evaluative and diagnostic activities. Hoffman continues in his paper, "In work adjustment, the objectives are to determine the success or failure of the adjustment plan to determine when to terminate the work adjustment process. Prevocational, vocational and work evaluation are assessment processes, and work adjustment (while evaluation does take place during the process) is a treatment process" (Hoffman, 1972).

Gefland sees work adjustment as *the next logical step* in the work evaluation procedure: "Work adjustment, then, is an intensified continuation of the process of work evaluation. It utilizes such principles as 1) sharing the diagnosis with the disabled client, i.e., bringing to his attention his positive and negative work habits and attitudes through the observation of work behavior as manifested by his production of work and his behavioral approach to work, 2) working through faulty work patterns through consistent interpretation of them, 3) offering encouragement to improve poor habits, and 4) providing rewards when improvement occurs (Gefland, 1966).

John G. Cull, co-author with Richard E. Hardy of *Standards in Evaluation,* in an article in *Vocational Evaluation and Work Adjustment Bulletin* published in 1969, has suggested certain steps in the total work evaluation and work adjustment area which offer help in distinguishing the various activities of the process. The four steps listed are:

1. Prevocational evaluation: An activity which provides the very basic behaviors for an individual to be a member of our culture, e.g., personal grooming, eating and other activities of daily living, etc.
2. Work adjustment: An activity in which the client begins to focus on general work skills and begins to learn the necessary work habits relating to attendance, punctuality, employer-employee relationships and employee-employee relationships—those activities that are common to all jobs.
3. Work evaluation: This step follows a decision which is made after the work adjustment program has ended: whether the client has the potential and the appropriate motivation to move into the world of work; or because of severity of disability, will become active in an *activity center* type program established to provide productive work.

Cull suggests that a work evaluation program will offer an opportunity for evaluation or adjustment training in the specific skills and in a more reality-oriented approach in terms of job tryouts, etc. It is at this point that the client begins to move toward vocational placement (Cull, 1972).

In reviewing statements by leaders in the field, it is clear that, while some confusion does exist in definition and description, all appear to be in agreement with Hoffman that work adjustment is a distinctive maneuver in the total evaluation and adjustment plan for the handicapped person and that work adjustment training is a *treatment process utilizing work or aspects of work to modify behavior* (Hoffman, 1972).

In addition, the staff of the Work Adjustment Project at the University of Minnesota define work adjustment somewhat differently in a rather bold effort to provide the profession with a theory of work adjustment. "Work adjustment is defined as a function of the degree of correspondence (agreement) between an individual and his work environments." The individual brings to the job certain occupational abilities and vocational needs (preferences for specific reinforcing or rewarding conditions in jobs). The job, in turn, has certain ability requirements and offers opportunities for workers to gain specific reinforcers (e.g., money, social status, and security). The level of correspondence between the abilities of the individual and the ability requirements of his job is referred to as *satisfactoriness.* The level of correspondence between the vocational needs (preference) of an individual and the reinforcer systems of his job is referred to as *satisfaction.* Satisfaction and satisfactoriness are both related to tenure (remaining on the job or in an occupation). If satisfactoriness is sufficiently low, the worker is fired or demoted. If satisfaction is sufficiently low, the worker will quit the job." The statement of this theory or definition of work adjustment is clear and parsimonious and appears to provide one base in the establishment of what Lofquist calls a *tentative frame of reference* (Lofquist, 1969). And while all definitions of work adjustment have application to the establishment of work adjustment programs for the deaf, Lofquist, in a recent article in the *Journal of Rehabilitation of the Deaf,* has shown how the Work Adjustment Project's theory can be applied specifically to adjustment problems of deaf people. He points out two of the special questions that he feels must be answered relative to the application of his theory to the problems of deaf people:

"1. With appropriate abilities for certain specific jobs, can the individual communicate his capacity successfully enough to be judged satisfactory, as he should, or does special provision need to be made?

"2. If the job reinforcers (satisfiers) match the individual's psychological needs, will they be perceived by the individual, or does some tailoring of the administration of rewards need to be done so that they will be perceived and the deaf worker will be satisfied with the job?" (Lofquist, 1970).

The central uniqueness in deaf people's work adjustment is, of course, the problem of communication. But, the deaf person also approaches a work adjustment program with an education that is, in many instances, a greater disability than his deafness. Low levels of adjustment in a formal or informal program of work adjustment comes about as a result of a grossly inadequate educational system, according to Vernon: "While rehabilitation has made giant steps to overcome the problem, educational programs at the federal level are actually supporting the outdated and the ineffective while ignoring the deaf community and constructive programs" (Vernon, 1970). Vernon suggests additional facilities be established to provide work programs for deaf youth, including those who are multiply-handicapped.

The results of one study indicates that the vocational development of deaf adolescents differs from that of hearing adolescents whose vocational adjustment is seen to be the end result of a developmental process. This research used a modified Career Pattern Study (an instrument developed for hearing adolescents by Donald Super) and the findings suggested that existing programs for training and orientation have little impact on deaf adolescents. "Rehabilitation services must develop channels for increasing information, changing attitudes, and developing potentials, particularly at early ages" (Adler, 1970).

There are several demonstration projects related to the deaf person's adjustment to work. One, reported in *Rehabilitation Record,* is located at Central Ohio Goodwill Industries in Columbus. Project DEAF (Diagnostic, Evaluation and Adjustment Facility) attempts to integrate all activities in a work evaluation and work adjustment program into a reality oriented program. Deaf clients spend each morning at some particular job for work tolerance and work adjustment. Other aspects of the program include remedial training, special educational assistance with writing and math, sex education and instruction in sign language for those who need this skill. John Caprio, Assistant Director, in commenting on the success of the project, said "It appears that fifty-seven people are now employed who were not previously employed, and, that is a success" (Wade, 1970). A steering committee sponsored by the Social and Rehabilitation Service Administration and the Arkansas Rehabilitation Research Training Center has recommended that Congress authorize the establishment of comprehensive centers to meet the needs of low (under) achieving deaf people. The report of this committee's national conference made the following specific recommendation for a work adjustment program as a major component of the center: "A work adjustment training program will be designed to facilitate the learning of basic work habits and skills, work attitudes, constructive relationships with co-workers and supervisors, and the concepts and language basic to all productive employment. This program will be carried out in a setting that is a simulated work environment, with attractive, well structured work tasks that provide rewards to the client that will reinforce learning" (Arkansas Rehabilitation Research and Training Center, 1971).

Douglas Burke of the National Institute for the Deaf at Rochester Institute of Technology in New York states that the rehabilitation counselor is in a unique position to assist the large number of deaf people who suffer in some degree from mental illness or emotional problems. "The vocational rehabilitation program will uncover a number of hardcore emotional problems that call for solution before case services can become effective. Existing service gaps can be bridged if the counselor can find the time to build the bridges" (Burke, 1969). In Burke's outline of several areas of need, he emphasized the potential for emotional growth in group work or what he called *sensitivity training*. He felt that, with proper training, rehabilitation staff could become facilitators of small groups of deaf clients—with selection of participants left to the judgment of the facilitator: all deaf persons, a mixture of deaf and hard of hearing people, or a mixture of deaf clients and leaders from the deaf community. The goal would be for deaf clients to develop a deeper awareness of themselves and the impact that they make on other people, as well as a better insight into emotional problems related to their own feeling with respect to getting along with the hearing population (Burke, 1969).

A description of a work adjustment program appears in the *Rehabilitation Counseling Bulletin.* Richard J. Baker, who is associated with the Rehabilitation Facility In-Service Training Project, Auburn University's well known program in work adjustment, lists six general techniques included in the program. On group counseling as a technique in work adjustment for handicapped clients, he lists several advantages and disadvantages experienced in group work for adjustment purposes. While these will not be listed here since they represent fairly universal and general problems in all group counseling endeavors, it seems important to direct attention to one of those disadvantages named: "Many clients in rehabilitation facilities have poor communication skills and group counseling is not particularly effective with nonverbal clients" (Baker, 1972). This disadvantage of group counseling in work adjustment centers, as experienced by many of the professionals, illustrates also the greater problem that can be expected in group counseling with deaf clients.

Group Counseling—One Approach for Deaf People in Adjustment to Work

Group counseling in rehabilitation can be defined as the process in which the counselor (or other rehabilitation adjustment personnel) and a small group (eight to ten members) of clients work together in order for the clients to acquire more normal developmental tasks and prepare for a more satisfactory adjustment to life through productive activity—it includes, then, the cognitive as well as the affective areas, and the desired outcomes represent a confluence of these two aspects of behavioral change.

Walter Neff, in his book *Work and Human Behavior,* chronicles the shift in work adjustment techniques from *guidance* to *counseling* in more recent times as rehabilitation staff have turned to the problems of the more severely handicapped person (and, deafness is classified by the Rehabilitation Services Administration as one of the severely handicapping conditions which provides an extension of time from six to eighteen months for evaluation related to feasibility of services); and, which Neff states implies an increasing belief that the problems of adjustment to work are in some sense or other, problems of personality. "Where these problems are severe, they cannot be solved by the giving of occupational information or the administration of tests. Some type of reconstruction of relevant areas of the personality appears to be required. The result has been an increasingly intensive search for appropriate methods of treatment" (Neff, 1968).

One method which this search has produced is group counseling, which is rapidly becoming ubiquitous in many of the centers and facilities serving deaf clients. The procedures or techniques used in these group counseling sessions range *from* large groups (resembling classrooms), participating in problem solving and task oriented assignments, with the work adjustment person viewed as an authoritative person—a teacher, a director of personnel, etc. *to* the small group approach based on Carl Rogers' basic encounter groups or other small group activities based exclusively in the affective area, with the work adjustment person acting as a group leader or facilitator utilizing extremely non-directive or group centered attitudes as well as techniques (Rogers, 1970). Rehabilitation personnel have participated for many years in the T-group or sensitivity training method developed by the National Training Laboratory in Bethel, Maine; and a few have developed relationships with trainers in order to provide sensitivity training to clients (hopefully, under close supervision). Other group training experiences include *The La Jolla Program* at the University of California at San Diego or Wake Forest University in Winston-Salem, North Carolina (sponsored by Carl Rogers and the Center for the Studies of the Person at La Jolla, California); Albert Ellis' marathon institutes in New York City in rational, emotive group therapy; and, available to rehabilitation staff in many parts of the country at this time are the Gestalt Therapy Group Sessions based on the small group practice of the Esalen Institute in Big Sur, California.

Two reasons for the emergence of a group counseling method

in many of the work adjustment centers are 1) the lack of staff to serve the large number of more severely handicapped people, the economic situation, and, 2) the prolific research writings in social psychology and its massive distribution of findings to the public and especially to professionals in educational settings.

Articles appearing in current rehabilitation journals indicate that group counseling is combined with individualized instruction and counseling by personnel involved in the total work evaluation and work adjustment process; and, that soon or eventually, either in individual sessions or in the group itself, work goals are introduced. As Walter Neff states, "One of the major requirements of the adjustment to work is the ability to interact in certain appropriate ways with other people present on the scene" (Neff, 1968). No rehabilitation worker with experience with deaf people will argue with this statement.

The Use of Group Techniques With Deaf Persons is a report of a workshop held last year at New York University's Deafness Research and Training Center. The editors indicate that group counseling for deaf persons, as viewed from the many disciplines represented in the book, *not only appears feasible, but also appears successful.* They conclude with a statement of concern regarding the need for professional people *to know more about the dynamics of deaf persons in groups with other deaf and with hearing members . . . deafness does not rule out the use of group techniques, neither when all members or when only some of the group are deaf. Having said that, however, it is also necessary to add that we need to learn more about the process as it involves deaf participants* (Schein and Naiman, 1971).

A review of the literature in the use of group counseling approaches for work adjustment programs for deaf people demonstrates that research is meager, and conclusive results apparently non-existent. The descriptive articles appearing in journals and monographs indicate that counselors, psychologists and other therapists are applying the various techniques of group psychotherapy as outlined earlier in this chapter to the small groups of deaf people—according to the therapist's past training and experience. The successful facilitator of a small group of deaf people appears to have an aptitude for making some desirable discoveries by accident, i.e., serendipity. Dr. Larry Stewart's doctoral dissertation (University of Arizona, 1969) is recommended by reviewers of research in this area: *Perceptions of Selected Variables of the Counseling Relationship in Group Counseling with Deaf College Students* (Schein and Naiman, 1971).

For the reader who has some training and some experience in one of the basic group counseling approaches in a rehabilitation setting *and,* is highly motivated to learn to work with deaf people, the following suggestions are made.

SUGGESTIONS FOR THE USE OF GROUP COUNSELLING IN WORK ADJUSTMENT FOR PEOPLE WHO ARE DEAF

Essential Prerequisites

1. *Read* the literature available on deafness. Valuable sources include: The Office of Deafness and Communicative Disorders, Rehabilitation Services Administration, Social and Rehabilitation Service, Department of Health, Education and Welfare, Washington, D. C.; The National Association of the Deaf, 814 Thayer Avenue, Silver Spring, Maryland 20910 (near Washington, D. C.); Gallaudet College Publications on Deafness Department, Kendall Green, Washington, D. C.; State Bureaus or Divisions of Vocational Rehabilitation and Graduate Programs in Rehabilitation Counseling.
2. *Contact* people who represent the *deaf community*—deaf people, parents in various professions who have a deaf child, the professional people who work with deaf people including the rehabilitation counselors and teachers of deaf people, ministers, priests, and rabbis, and others. Become a member of the *deaf community.*
3. Learn the language of the deaf. The National Association of the Deaf (address above) can furnish all materials needed and can also advise of community classes as well as furnish the names of interpreters.
4. If possible, solicit the help of a deaf person who is in a professional position in rehabilitation. His consultation and active participation later in the small group process will be most helpful.

Guidelines

1. Select four to eight deaf people for the small group who have received all necessary services through rehabilitation programs and who are now *ready* for a work adjustment program. You may want to give consideration to age, sex, personality type, etc.; however, the major criterion for selection is the *readiness* of the client for this experience, as perceived by you and other members of the rehabilitation staff, e.g., the psychologist, the work evaluator, and others.
2. Select two to five hearing people (not to exceed a total of ten members, when combined with the deaf members). Thesis: Deaf people are in need of relating to hearing people in the world of work—why wait?
3. Establish a ten week schedule which will include in the beginning four weeks of group counseling at one and one-half hours for each session; during the fifth week, arrange for individual conferences with the deaf and hearing members of the group; following four more weeks of one and a half hour group counseling sessions, use the tenth week for each client to develop a vocational plan with you during an individual counseling session. (It is recommended that you begin with an emphasis on interpersonal relationships or the affective area of learning; and, provide during the final weeks an opportunity for emphasis on information giving, job planning and other activities in the cognitive area of learning—obviously, all these suggestions are made as flexible guidelines, with recognition that your work environment or your own theory of group counseling will require that *you* be the judge of what is best for the deaf people who are your clients.)

The activities that are involved with the feelings of deaf people and those that are emphasizing thoughts and ideas that will lead to action are to be viewed as a more complete program of learning which will provide the deaf person with the interpersonal skills and with the knowledge about work which will help him toward a more productive and freer lifestyle. George Isaac Brown defines this blending as follows: "Confluent education is the term for the integration or flowing together of the affective and cognitive elements in individual and group learning, sometimes called humanistic or psychological education, a philosophy and a process of learning in which the affective domain and cognitive domain flow together like two streams merging into one river and are thus integrated in individual and group learning. It should be apparent that there is no intellectual learning without some sort of feeling, and there are no feelings without the mind's being somehow involved" (Brown, 1971).

The conclusion of this chapter comes with an awareness of its incompleteness—the lack of time and space to relate the aggregate of significant experiences in the field of deafness, to deal effectively with the ambiguity inherent in the whole area of group counseling in rehabilitation settings; and, to communicate an adequate procedure in the nebulous world of *work adjustment* which can be helpful to deaf people, many of whom are in great need of this aspect of the rehabilitation process. There may be, for us, some comfort in these words from Carl Rogers:

> "For it is not upon the physical sciences that the future will depend. It is upon us who are trying to understand and deal with the interaction between human beings—who are trying to create helping relationships." (Rogers, 1970)

REFERENCES

Adler, Edna P. (Ed.): *Research Trends in Deafness—State of the Art,* Department of Health, Education and Welfare, Social and Rehabilitation Service, Washington, D. C., June, 1970.

Baker, Richard J.: Determining the goals and techniques of adjustment services, *Rehabil Counsel Bull,* American Rehabilitation Counseling Association, Vol. 6, No. 1, September, 1972, pp. 29-39.

Brown, George Isaac: *Human Teaching for Human Learning, An Introduction to Confluent Education,* New York, Viking Press, 1971.

Burke, Douglas: Vocational rehabilitation and emerging mental health needs of the deaf, *Mental Health and the Deaf,* Altshuler, Kenneth Z., and Rainer, John D. (Eds.), Rehabilitation Services Administration, Social and Rehabilitation Service, Department of Health, Education and Welfare, 1969.

Comprehensive Regional Rehabilitation Centers for Low (Under) Achieving Deaf People: The Task Force Committee, sponsored by the Social and Rehabilitation Service and the Arkansas Rehabilitation Research Training Center, 1971.

Cull, John G.: Statements made during a personal interview at his office,

Regional Counselor Training Program, Virginia Commonwealth University, Woodrow Wilson Rehabilitation Center, Fishersville, Virginia, August 3, 1972.

Fant, Louie J.: Ameslan—*An Introduction to American Sign Language,* National Association of the Deaf, Silver Spring, Maryland, 1972.

Hoffman, Paul R.: Work evaluation: an overview, *Work Evaluation and Work Adjustment for Rehabilitation Services,* Cull, John G. and Hardy, Richard E. (Eds.), Springfield, Charles C Thomas, Publisher, 1972.

Locke, Mary Ann: Statements made during a personal interview at her office at the National Association of the Deaf, 814 Thayer Avenue, Silver Spring, Maryland, October 13, 1972.

Lofquist, Lloyd and Dawis, Rene V.: *Adjustment to Work,* New York, Appleton-Century-Crofts, 1969.

Lofquist, Lloyd: The general requirements of work. *J Rehabil, 2:*28-36, February, 1970.

Mindel, Eugene D. and Vernon, McCay: *They Grow in Silence,* National Association of the Deaf, Silver Spring, Maryland, 1971.

Neff, Walter S.: *Work and Human Behavior,* New York, Atherton Press, 1968.

Patterson, C. H. and Steward, Larry G.: Principles of counseling with deaf people, *Counseling With Deaf People,* Deafness Research and Training Center, New York University, Allen E. Sussman and Larry G. Stewart (Eds.), 1971.

Rogers, Carl R.: The characteristics of a helping relationship, *Models and Functions of Counseling—For Applied Settings and Rehabilitation Workers,* Bozarth, Jerold D. (Ed.), Social and Rehabilitation Service, Department of Health, Education and Welfare, July 1970.

Schein, Jerome D. and Naiman, Doris W. (Eds.): *The Use of Group Techniques With Deaf Persons,* New York University Deafness Research and Training Center, 1971.

Vernon, McCay: Crises of the deaf. *J Rehabil,* pp. 31-39 (November-December, 1971).

Wade, Barbara A.: Ohio's project DEAF, *Rehabilitation Record,* September-October, 1970, Rehabilitation Services Administration, U. S. Department of Health, Education and Welfare, pp. 7-8.

Williams, Boyce R. and Sussman, Allen E.: Social and psychological problems of deaf people, *Counseling With Deaf People,* Deafness Research and Training Center, New York University, Edited by Allen E. Sussman and Larry G. Stewart, 1971.

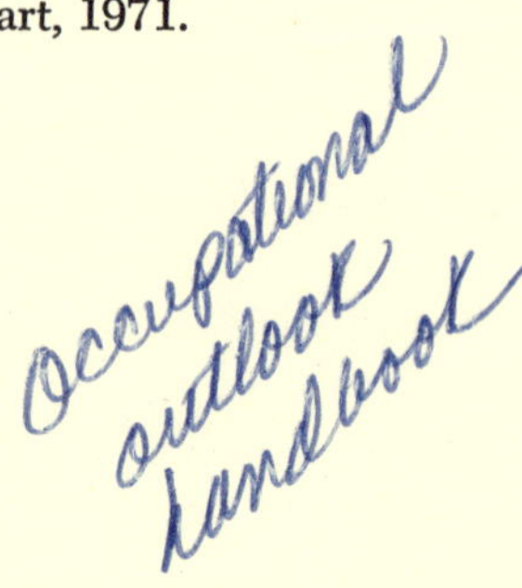

Chapter IX

PROGRESS THROUGH RESEARCH 1958 to 1972

THE DRF STORY

The Centurion Club
DRF Sponsored Research
DRF Indirect Grants
Educational Programs
The Future
DRF's Goal

*Probably no chronic physical impairment is as prevalent in the United States today as ear disorders.**

IT IS ESTIMATED that one out of every ten Americans has some degree of hearing loss or other communicative impairment. Many deaf adults are unable to realize their potentialities in a career, and the 15 per cent of the deafened who are children usually cannot obtain the normal education required to become self sufficient adults, capable of making their contributions to society.

The social as well as the human considerations of this are great, yet in 1958, the year DRF was founded, only one per cent of the annual expenditure for all medical research in the Unit-

* From a speech made from the floor of the Senate by Senator Lister Hill, at the time he requested that the Citation of The Alexander Graham Bell Association, honoring Mrs. Hobart C. Ramsey, be printed in the *Congressional Record.*

ed States was devoted to investigations of deafness and disorders of the ear.

During the years 1958 through 1971, the Deafness Research Foundation directed $3.7 million to otolaryngological research and related objectives.

The Deafness Research Foundation was established by Mrs. Hobart C. Ramsey, whose interest in otological research is deep and personal. In 1952, after many years of living with a severe hearing impairment, she was successfully operated on by the late Dr. Julius Lempert, who performed the then newly developed fenestration operation in both her ears.

Mrs. Ramsey was unwilling to take her return to the world of sound for granted, and she set about to establish an organization to advance otolaryngological research. Nothing like this had ever been attempted before and, in this pioneer work, she enlisted the interest and support of scientific, industrial and civic leaders.

The establishment of The Deafness Research Foundation brought to reality her driving determination to form a national organization that would make a concentrated voluntary effort toward the following objectives: 1) arouse the public and alert United States industry and private philanthropy to the needs of ear research; 2) encourage more research scientists to focus attention in this field; 3) provide a central source of information necessary for coordination of research and 4) raise funds to support research and conduct public and professional educational programs.

Shortly thereafter these objectives were enlarged to include the awarding of the *seed money* grants that make it possible for promising young investigators to enter the field of otolaryngological research.

The Deafness Research Foundation is endorsed by leading medical organizations, including the American Otological Society, Inc., American Laryngological, Rhinological and Otological Society, Inc., American Academy of Ophthalmology and Otolaryngology and Section on Laryngology, and Otology and Rhinology of the American Medical Association.

DRF is not a private foundation within the meaning of the

Tax Reform Act of 1969. Its support comes largely from tax exempt voluntary contributions from individuals, foundations, corporations and the Centurion Coub.

THE CENTURION CLUB

In 1963, the medical profession expressed its confidence in The Deafness Research Foundation by forming the Centurion Club. The goal of this organization of ear, nose, and throat physicians, their professional societies and allied specialists, is to underwrite the operating costs of The Deafness Research Foundation through annual membership dues, thus enabling DRF to make available other gifts for research and related objectives.

Starting with a nucleus of nineteen members, this altruistic organization has grown steadily and, by the end of 1971, had a membership of some 1,200. The Centurion Club of DRF is unique, for physicians in no other area of medicine support a voluntary health agency to such an extent.

In addition to their financial support, individual Centurion Club members have assisted the Temporal Bone Banks Program for Ear Research (see below) by aiding in the dissemination of informational material through all media. They have presented the work and objectives of DRF to their patients, as well as to many public and professional audiences.

Beverly W. Armstrong, M.D., of Charlotte, North Carolina, is currently serving a two year term as Centurion Club president. In this office he was preceded by George E. Shambaugh, Jr. (1963), Howard P. House (1964), J. V. D. Hough (1965), J. B. Farrior (1966), Francis A. Sooy (1967), John E. Bordley (1968), C. V. Kinney (1969), and Shirley H. Baron (1970). All the foregoing are outstanding physicians in the field of otolaryngology. A listing of the full Centurion Club membership appears annually in the Fall issue of DRF's newsletter, the *Receiver*.

DRF SPONSORED RESEARCH

I. The Temporal Bone Banks Program For Ear Research

In 1960, a major problem facing otological researchers was the fact that the inner ear, due to its inaccessible location within the temporal bone, could not be examined during life.

The importance of temporal bones to otological research had long been recognized by investigators in the field. As early as the 1920's, several laboratories in the United States were studying the pathology of temporal bones.

Throughout the 1950's the medical profession, and particularly various committees of the American Academy of Ophthalmology and Otolaryngology (AAOO) were increasingly interested in the study of temporal bones and had taken steps to disseminate knowledge to the profession on the procedures for removal and preparation of temporal bones and, hopefully, to find some means of collecting them systematically.

To meet this challenge The Deafness Research Foundation, led by Mrs. Ramsey, worked with members of the AAOO, through the Academy's Committee for the Conservation of Hearing, to launch The Temporal Bone Banks Program for ear research to provide qualified researchers with a source of bequeathed inner ears for scientific investigation.

Due to its central location, the first Temporal Bone Banks Center was established at the University of Chicago, to function in collaboration with The Deafness Research Foundation and the American Academy of Ophthalmology and Otolaryngology. Subsequently three other regional centers were established at the University of California, San Francisco; Baylor University, Houston; and The Johns Hopkins University, Baltimore.

All funds used for the inauguration of the TBB Program, as well as the establishment and first year costs of the four regional centers, were raised through DRF by Mrs. Ramsey, who personally was able to influence various foundations and corporations to make substantial contributions for these specific purposes.

In 1966, the Armed Forces Institute of Pathology (AFIP) affiliated with the TBB Program for Ear Research. One set of slides for microscopic study from each significant specimen processed is now sent to AFIP from the thirty-eight ear banks and laboratories throughout the country who are working with the program, processing specimens and conducting research. At AFIP these slides become part of the nation's central registry for ear pathology, available for correlative studies by interested ear researchers and for instructional purposes.

Without a joint partnership involving the coordination of both private and public financial support, the growth of the Temporal Bone Banks Program would not have achieved the degree of success it has experienced. It is also significant to note that the federal government recognized the importance of the TBB Centers early in the life of the Program, and provided for their maintenance from the second year through 1971, when it became evident that many advantages, both technical and educational, would be found in the consolidation of the four regional centers into one national center serving the entire nation. Among these would be the opportunity for the program to conduct new teaching and training courses designed to upgrade the technical level of TBB research.

Consequently, in January, 1972, the four regional centers were consolidated into *The National Temporal Bone Banks Center of The Deafness Research Foundation,* located in The Johns Hopkins University Hospital, Baltimore, and operated under the joint sponsorship of DRF, AAOO, and AFIP. The Deafness Research Foundation has pledged itself to underwrite the Center's first year operating costs.

Accomplishment of the TBB Program

Surveys made in 1971 indicate that there were then in excess of ten thousand documented bequests of temporal bones.

Approximately one thousand sets of temporal bones have been processed in participating temporal bone laboratories. The majority of these bones were obtained by the public education programs conducted on a national basis by The Deafness Research Foundation.

There have been 144 reports published in leading American medical journals on research projects conducted by laboratories in the TBB Program.

Additional information on the Temporal Bone Banks Program for Ear Research and forms for bequeathing inner ears for research will be sent upon request to DRF.

II. DRF Grants Program

The Deafness Research Foundation awards a grant once a year for a project period beginning January 1. Contingent upon the satisfactory development of the project, a continuation application may be submitted for a second and third year renewal.

Medical research funded by The Deafness Research Foundation is conducted at leading institutions in the United States and Canada. The following is a brief summary of progress made through DRF sponsored research during the years 1958 to 1972.

A. Conductive Hearing Loss

One of the Deafness Research Foundation's first grants, in 1959, sponsored a scientific investigation on otosclerosis with conductive hearing loss. Since that time new surgical techniques for the treatment of otosclerosis, from the Lempert fenestration operation to the present procedures predicated on a direct approach to the fixed stapes foot plate, have evolved. Today over 90 per cent of *suitable* patients can benefit from such operations.

Otosclerosis. Over the years DRF has continued to sponsor research on otosclerosis with conductive loss, and studies concerned with the microchemical assay of the fluorine content in normal and otosclerotic bone after sodium fluoride treatment, as well as the evaluation of chromosomal abnormality in otosclerosis, have also been supported.

Conductive Hearing Loss: Secondary to Infection. In recent years, investigations on conductive hearing losses secondary to infection and adhesive processes have received increasing attention and support by the Deafness Research Foundation. The Temporal Bone Banks Program for Ear Research has made unique contributions to the knowledge of the pathologic processes existing in the middle ear and mastoid bone in chronic infection. From this basic knowledge the concept of modern tympanoplastic surgery has evolved.

Tympanoplasty. Investigations sponsored by The Deafness Research Foundation have carried out experimental tympanoplastic procedures, and attempts have been made to repair total ear drum perforations using vein to cover the perforations.

DRF is currently supporting research to determine the safety and usefulness of tissue adhesives and steroids in tympanoplasty, and to learn if these tissue adhesives (polymerizing substances) used in the repositioning of ossicles in the middle ear cavity can be tolerated safely.

Ossicle Dislocation. Ossicular chain discontinuity as an accidental finding in conductive deafness has been observed in histologic sections studied in DRF's Temporal Bone Banks Laboratories. Exploratory operations on the middle ear for conductive hearing loss have also revealed many instances of ossicular chain discontinuity. Re-establishment of the integrity of the ossicular chain can result in dramatic improvement in the hearing.

Stapedectomy. The Deafness Research Foundation has supported investigations on the effect of bleeding into the perilymphatic space during stapedectomy. The products of the breakdown of blood were removed from the perilymphatic space, mainly via a thin walled capillary mesh. Bleeding into the labyrinth explains, in part, how high tone loss may be present in patients who have undergone successful operations for otosclerosis.

Serous Otitis Media. Much needs to be learned with respect to the function of the eustachian tube and its effect on hearing. Malfunction of the tube has been regarded as a cause of serous otitis media with resultant hearing losses.

Five DRF sponsored research projects are being carried out to determine experimentally: a) the effects of ligation of the eustachian tube; b) causes of seromucinous otitis media; c) microbiology of recurrent serous otitis media; d) results of the establishment of an eustachian tube mastoid antrum maxillary sinus shunt and, finally, e) the significant etiologic factors in serous otitis media and the role that the lymphatics play.

In the past, serous otitis media has been treated surgically with a tonsil and adenoid operation and, at times, with the insertion of a polyethylene tube into the middle ear cavity. Too often these procedures have failed to re-establish normal hearing, and it is hoped that the DRF research investigations now underway will bring new insight into the problems resulting from serous otitis media.

Cholesteatoma. Cholesteatoma, that complication of chronic middle ear infection often causing a conductive hearing loss, is becoming increasingly frequent in young people.

The Deafness Research Foundation is currently supporting scientific investigations that are studying the mechanism of deafness produced by this type of infection, the face of infected middle ear epithelium and if, or how, squamous metaplasia from mucosal epithelial cells takes place. Another DRF sponsored investigation, on the origin of collagenase in middle ear cholesteatoma, should shed light on the mechanism of the destruction of vital structures of the ear, with resultant hearing loss.

B. Sensori-Neural Hearing Loss

Any consideration of sensori-neural hearing loss must take into account its many varied causes. Over the years, The Deafness Research Foundation has funded projects which may, directly or indirectly, contribute to the ultimate solution of this problem.

Basic Research. To fill in the gaps in our knowledge of the cochlea and its central connections, DRF has supported research to investigate the protein components of perilymph in normal and pathological ears and the pharmacology of audition with specific reference to the cochlea inhibitory (olivo-cochlea) tract.

Prospects of significant progress have been heightened by the availability of modern equipment. The work that first utilized stereo and phase contrast microscopy on premature and full term infant temporal bones was funded with a grant from The Deafness Research Foundation.

DRF has also supported basic research designed to minimize autolytic changes in the temporal bone; perfect a rapid method of decalcifying the temporal bone; improve techniques that now make it possible to bypass the older, time consuming methods.

Acoustic Neuroma. A grant from DRF supported a study of the blood supply of the inner ear and the cerebello-pontine angle in relation to acoustic tumors, a lesion not an uncommon cause of sensori-neural hearing loss. This investigation made a significant contribution to the development of a new, widely acclaimed surgical technique for the cure of acoustic neuroma.

Viral Deafness. A DRF sponsored investigation, working on viruses in the inner ear, resulted in perfecting an important new procedure for studying tissues. When routine frozen sections failed to provide the cellular detail needed for identification of the viruses by phase and fluorescent microscopy, the investigator devised a freeze substitution method whereby tissue fluid is converted into ice crystals that occupy a volume no greater than the original fluid. Cellular structures are not exploded when defrosted. The histology is precise. Intracellular viral particles are stationary, and the distortion seen in former routine histologic techniques does not occur.

One of DRF's earliest grants in 1962 was made to study the sensori-neural auditory pathology in humans. With the development of three dimensional microscopy, and with the availability of precise motion picture photographic equipment, it is now possible to observe the passage of blood cells through the capillary vessels of the basilar membrane. DRF has sponsored microelectrode studies of the energy transformation process that takes place in the organ of Corti in relation to the changes in this blood supply brought about by various agents known to produce sensori-neural hearing loss.

Cochlear Otosclerosis. Current DRF support is being given to ongoing research projects studying minerals in normal and otosclerotic stapes. Use of a nondispersive x-ray analyzer attached to a scanning electron microscope makes possible a critical analysis of mineral distribution in the undecalcified stapes. Otosclerosis in patients with genetically determined sensori-neural deafness is rarely mentioned in the literature, but a DRF sponsored study has demonstrated that this combination of conditions does occur.

Other DRF supported investigations have also studied vascular shunts, occasionally observed in cochlear otosclerosis, to determine if these are significant factors in causation.

Ototoxic Drugs. The eighth nerve, especially the cochlear branch, has long been known to be susceptible to many drugs. With the use of newer drugs and antibiotics, severe ototoxic effects have become increasingly frequent.

The Deafness Research Foundation has supported studies on the effects of: a) streptomycin, neomycin and kanamycin on the vestibular apparatus in experimental animals; b) ethacrynic acid on the cochlea and vestibular apparatus and c) gentamycin ototoxicity. Precisely how these drugs produce sensori-neural hearing loss (usually irreversible) in some individuals has yet to be determined. Much scientific investigation must still be done in this area.

Rubella, Measles and Mumps. Impressive histologic data demonstrating the disastrous effect of rubella, measles and mumps on the cochlea has emerged from work carried out in the laboratories affiliated with DRF's Temporal Bone Banks Program for Ear Research. In an epidemiologic sense, in rubella, children constitute the major portion of the *herd* of susceptibles that the virus requires to maintain itself in the population, and elevation of *herd immunity* is the only approach offering hope of altering the epidemiologic cycle of rubella.

Since 1969, through its public education facilities and professional affiliations, the Deafness Research Foundation has been cooperating with the *Stop Rubella* immunization campaign of the Public Health Service.

Meniere's Disease. Many possible etiologies of Meniere's disease have been advanced. The Deafness Research Foundation has supported investigations of Meniere's disease concerned with: a) oxygen tension of inner ear fluids; b) effect of anaphylactic shock and associated increased endolymphatic fluid pressure changes on the organ of Corti and c) distribution of Na^{22} and K^{42} in tissue and fluid spaces of cochlea related to the time of injection of the isotopes. Such projects have broadened knowledge of the fluid dynamics of the inner ear, and the passage of identifiable tagged ions in inner ear fluids has been observed and confirmed in another DRF supported investigation. There is question that faulty endolymph absorption, as well as endolymphatic hydrops, may be factors in Meniere's disease.

Future research will, hopefully, clarify the mechanisms of the development and absorption of endolymphatic fluid, and shed light on the utility of the numerous surgical procedures currently used on the endolymphatic sac to stop the attacks of Meniere's dizziness and preserve residual hearing.

A recent DRF sponsored scientific investigation is designed to determine the harmful effects, if any, of cryotherapy to the harmful effects, if any of cryotherapy to the inner ear (via the round window membrane) to prevent recurrent attacks of vertigo and more importantly, conserve residual hearing.

C. Genetic Deafness

Mindful of the multiplicity of problems involved in a meaningful attack on genetic deafness, the Deafness Research Foundation has supported studies on chromosomal abnormality and otopathologic findings in fetuses, newborns and premature infants. Research has been sponsored to develop non-surgical recording of human auditory nerve potentials and cochlear microphonics into a clinically useful procedure. DRF projects have studied the effect of intensity on the average electroencephalic response (AER) during sleep in the search for a successful clinical audiometric technique when the AER cannot be obtained by other methods.

Such investigations have now made it possible to detect congenital deafness in the newborn and, consequently, differentiate between congenital deafness and mental retardation.

The findings of a DRF sponsored project that coordinated the work of many disciplines (otolaryngology, histology, audiology, genetics and social services) provide convincing proof of the scientific benefits to be derived from a team effort in long term studies of genetics deafness.

DRF scientific investigations have also contributed substantially to the development of a successful organ culture system in the laboratory, with subsequent electron microscopic studies of organ culture specimens that determine if ultrastructural features are developing in such a way as to indicate that the organ culture system can be regarded as a true model. Other aspects of this work are found in the experiments in ototoxicity and fetal viral infections designed to throw light on how congenital malformations occur.

Research supported by DRF has helped to establish the pleuri-directional tomography useful in establishing types of congenital abnormality (ossicle, ossicle absence, ossicle fusion, etc.). This procedure can now be used to indicate the nature of an abnormality prior to surgery.

A DRF supported study that correlated the pleuri-directional tomography findings with the histology of the temporal bone substantiated the reliability of this work.

D. Noise: Its Effect on Hearing

Investigations of hearing loss caused by noise have been sponsored by DRF, both by participating in the support of a research laboratory established by the Subcommittee on Noise, Committee of Conservation of Hearing, American Academy of Ophthalmology and Otolaryngology, and the awarding of grants for research in this area.

DRF sponsored studies on the effect of noise on hearing, and on the recovery from auditory fatigue produced by steady and interrupted noise exposure, have yielded valuable information on the ability of the eighth nerve to recover from noise trauma of known degree and duration.

The significance of temporary threshold shifts following exposure to intermittent noise with short bursts is the subject of a recent DRF investigation. Another DRF project studied sonic boom effects on the cochlea.

E. Presbycusis

DRF grants have been given for presbycusis investigations: a) neuro-anatomical correlates of speech discrimination; b) the degree of hearing loss in later life; c) histopathology of hearing and equilibrium disorders and d) the pathology of presbycusis.

Recently DRF supported a project to develop an animal model for the study of this condition. It is believed that such a model will be most useful in the study of the mechanisms of human presbycusis allowing, as it will, controlled experiments to test the validity of what have been, up to the present, only hypothesized theories on the causes of presbycusis.

It is hoped that current work will shed light on the effect of diet, cholesterol, stress and noise on the production of changes in the inner ear, hitherto regarded as pathognomic of the aging process.

F. Neuro-Science

Within the context of this discussion the general term, neuroscience, is used to include the categories of neuro-anatomy, neuro-embryology and neuro-chemistry of the ear and its central connections.

Neuro-Anatomy. DRF has given support for neuro-science investigations on: a) the correlation of temporal bone pathology with functional changes in the auditory and vestibular systems; b) experimental studies of the efferent fibers of the eighth nerve; c) the role of the efferent cochlear innervation on hearing; d) the functional organization of afferent cochlear projections in primates and e) electron microscopic studies on the topographic synaptology of the hair cells of the vestibular organs.

A DRF sponsored study of cochlear innervation seeks to demonstrate how individual spiral ganglion cells innervate both inner and outer hair cells. The new technique used in this work, the rapid Golgi method, minimizes the need for sectioning and reconstruction thus eliminating many of the difficulties attendant on following a single cell and its processes.

Neuro-Chemistry. Work on the cytochemistry of the organ of Corti and the central auditory pathway, an area not previously explored, is being carried out under a grant from The Deafness Research Foundation. The investigators have quantitative, as well as qualitative, evidence of the localization of neuro-transmitters, acetylcholesterinase, butylcholesterinase and choline acetyl transferinase in the neurotubules and at synaptic organelles. It is hoped that results of such studies as this will clarify the manner of transmission of sound in the auditory pathway.

Neuro-Embryology. Although it is generally agreed that the study of the neuro-embryology of the inner ear provides insight into this complex organ, little work has been done in this area. The recent development of serial section electron microscopic techniques have lessened the problems inherent in such research, and DRF is currently supporting an investigation that is working on a three dimensional analysis of the development of the inner ear of the frog. The results of this study could cast light on how congenital deafness occurs.

Multidisciplinary Study of the Inner Ear. An investigation, utilizing the skills of a physicist, an otolaryngologist, a bio-medical engineer and a physiologist, is receiving DRF support to study Doppler shift measurements for a mathematical model of cochlear mechanics that will describe the detailed motion of the basilar membrane and its relation to neural activity of the spiral ganglion.

Other attempts at synthesizing a mathematical model have been made in the past, but none has had the self correcting techniques of this systems approach nor the use of instruments that are extremely sensitive and capable of measuring the movement of the basilar membrane. Involved in this project are anatomic studies using surface specimen techniques and graphic reconstructions, microelectrode measurements of the spiral ganglion and laser Doppler shift measurements of the basilar membrane movement.

DRF INDIRECT GRANTS

A DRF indirect grant is financial support made directly by a donor to a specified institution as the result of the efforts and intercession of the Deafness Research Foundation. Since its inception, in addition to direct grants, DRF has been responsible for substantial sums of money having been channeled to the support of ear research through these indirect grants.

EDUCATIONAL PROGRAMS

Publication Education. Using all forms of media, DRF's public education program has been directed to bringing about a greater awareness of the seriousness of deafness, urging regular ear examinations, and encouraging individuals with ear disorders to bequeath their inner ear structures to the Temporal Bone Banks Program for Ear Research.

Professional Education. To assist the dissemination of important ear research, DRF has co-sponsored and collaborated in two symposia:

Biochemical Mechanisms in Hearing and Deafness, University of Minnesota, 1968.

Otophysiology, University of Michigan, 1971.

THE FUTURE

Scientific knowledge accumulated through otolaryngological research in the years since the inception of The Deafness Research Foundation opens opportunities for advances inconceivable only a short time ago. Included among these are the following two examples of ongoing work with implications for the future:

Basic research studies now are being conducted on the use of electronic devices to transmit auditory impulses to the brain, bypassing the non-functioning inner ear. These investigations can have great significance as they could provide data that might justify the use of electronic devices, in suitable cases, to give sound to individuals now hopelessly deafened with far advanced or total nerve deafness.

Through technical experience gained in methods of preserving and distributing otologic tissue, ossicular and eardrum transplantation will have far greater availability to the medical profession in the future. Several tissue banks are already in operation, and some are distributing ear drums and middle ear bones for middle ear transplants on a nationwide basis.

DRF'S GOAL

The goal of The Deafness Research Foundation is to seek out the causes and improved means of prevention and treatment of deafness, and thus help to provide all mankind with the prospect of effective human communication.

Toward this end, The Deafness Research Foundation will continue to serve as a channel through which assistance can be provided by foundations, corporations, professional organizations and individual benefactors to advance all areas of otolaryngological research.

Chapter X

PRE-SCHOOL EDUCATION FOR DEAF CHILDREN

Helen S. Lane

Education for the deaf child should begin as soon as there is a diagnosis of hearing impairment. Early diagnosis and evaluation may require the services of professionals in various fields—pediatricians, otologists, audiologists, psychologists, teachers of the deaf, and social workers equipped to get all the necessary information about the child. The task of the counselor is one of involving the parents in an educational program based on the information about the child.

In 1964, a conference concerned with the identification and management of the young deaf child was held in Toronto, Canada. In a summary of the conference discussions, Davis (1964) stated that methods for routine screening of the newborn infant for auditory impairment have been developed but the incidence of hearing impairment in the newborn is low (the range in three extensive studies was from 0.1 per cent to 2.0 per cent) and the validity and reliability of screening tests are difficult to establish. An effective program for the early identification of children likely to have problems in communication can and should be instituted immediately by testing at three month intervals during the first year and six month intervals during the second year all children listed on a High Risk Register because the risk of an auditory handicap for these children is far greater than would be found in the general population. The success of referrals for such a testing program will depend upon the education of physicians, public health personnel and parents.

As soon as deafness is identified, the parents are in need of counselling. The confirmation of a hearing loss is a traumatic experience. The impact of a deaf child on his family is vividly and realistically described by Mindel and Vernon (1971). Anxiety, bewilderment and shock are followed by sorrow and feelings of guilt. Schlesinger and Meadow (1972) feel that parents of a child with a handicap want up-to-date and accurate scientific information about the child's condition. They want to know what they can do to help their child develop to his capacity and what they may expect this capacity to be.

Parents usually find their way to a Hearing and Speech Clinic for additional testing and more information. The case history gives the clinicians the first information about the child. It may be in the form of a questionnaire that can be mailed to the clinic or filled in with the assistance of a social worker.

The data in a case history according to Levine (1960) relate to genetic, somatic, and psychological facts of development, the socioeconomic, cultural and emotional climate of environment, and the major and minor motivations of behavior. Psychological tests give only present status and interview is limited because of communication obstacles. Therefore, psychologists must turn to case histories for major assistance in diagnostic appraisal of deaf persons. Levine (1960) has published the case history form she devised for deaf children and adults.

The hearing tests administered depend upon the age of the child and his cooperation. Electric response audiometry is a part of the routine hearing evaluation of all children under four years of age in the Hearing Clinics at Central Institute for the Deaf. If the child can be conditioned to respond to pure tones in play audiometry this is used to compare ERA estimates of threshold with behavioral thresholds.

An estimate of intelligence is another part of the clinical evaluation. Before the age of two, developmental scales such as the Gesell Developmental Schedules and the Bayley Scales may be used. Infant tests are not valid as predictors of I.Q. or school achievement, according to Thomas (1970).

After the age of two, mental tests that are non-verbal in administration and response may be used. Such tests should give a broad clinical picture and correlate with verbal tests of intelligence. The Randall's Island Performance Series (1930), the

Smith Non-Verbal Performance Scale (1960), the Snijders-Ooman Non-Verbal Scale (1959), or the Hiskey-Nebraska Test of Learning Aptitude (1966) meet the criteria for preschool age deaf children.

Measurement of the intelligence of a preschool deaf child should be considered an index of his ability in terms of normal or below or above average intelligence and not an exact I.Q. However, if all tests in the battery are below his chronological age, slow learning may be anticipated. In some tests there is great variability or spread of scores among the test items of the battery. This variability may be due to factors related to the child's handicap such as motor dexterity, memory span or eye-hand coordination.

Other factors to be considered in the interpretation of mental test scores at the time of evaluation are:

1. Fatigue of the child. Travel to the Hearing and Speech Clinic may necessitate very early departure from home, all night travel, an exciting first plane flight, or a first night in a motel. Test schedules may start with hearing tests that require attention and extended periods of inactivity leaving him restless for the psychometric tests.
2. Apprehension of the child. When the child is taken to a strange room, separated from his parents, even with the assurance that they are just outside waiting, he becomes anxious especially if the clinic is in a hospital and the psychometrist wears a white coat.
3. Many performance tests depend upon speed for scores and deaf children are not aware of the need to hurry.
4. Memory for test. Parents may be anxious to get more than one evaluation of their child and travel from clinic to clinic seeking impartial advice. Therefore, they do not mention previous test results. With the limited number of performance test items, children remember and perform with great speed and accuracy. An experienced psychometrist can detect this and shift to another test battery.

With the information obtained from the case history, the hearing tests, the mental tests and observation by an experienced teacher of the deaf of the vocalizations of the child, the counselling of parents begins. Mindel and Vernon (1971) feel that the persons who test hearing are pivotal in the deaf child's life and they advise parents without sufficient information about methods of instruction.

Schlesinger and Meadow (1972) feel that teachers must guard against usurping parents' *right to know* of differing approaches to the treatment of the handicapped child, and parents' *right to decide* about the treatment their child receives.

If the Hearing and Speech Clinic is part of an educational program, parents should be given an opportunity to observe deaf children in classes at all levels of instruction from beginning preschool to graduating classes. They can see how deaf children learn to communicate, how they acquire academic and vocational skills, and how they are prepared to fit into a hearing world. Parents should be urged to visit other schools and exercise their right to select the educational program they want for their deaf child.

For the preschool age deaf child the most important factor is loving, intelligent, and consistent parental care. In her talks to parents, Mrs. Tracy emphasized the value of those early months when the infant was in mother's arms and she talked close to its ear. The human voice, speaking loudly and clearly close to the ear can usually reach any significant residue of hearing. For this reason, parents must be urged to continue talking even after the diagnosis of deafness is confirmed.

Davis (1964) in his summary of the Toronto conference gives two precautions that must be observed concerning the use of amplified sound for infants:

1. The diagnosis of peripheral hearing loss must be clearly established. The reaction of the child, particularly indications of discomfort when the hearing aid is turned on, must be carefully observed and respected.
2. For children with fragmentary hearing for low frequencies only, hearing aids with extended low frequency range are more effective than aids with the usual response characteristic that favors high tones and attenuates the low.

Amplified sound, produced by a hearing aid, can now be provided to infants as young as six months. Some experts hesitate to put hearing aids on young babies whose exposure to sound will be uncontrolled and advise the use of amplification only under controlled conditions.

Parents must understand that hearing aids will not *restore* normal hearing. According to Hirsh (1970) the teacher hopes that amplified sound will yield for the deaf child information about voice intonation, syllabic and verbal segmentation, other aspects of rhythmic structure, and some discrimination of speech sounds based principally on the low frequency sounds that are audible.

Education of the deaf child starts in mother's arms, then moves to some type of parent-infant program where the experienced teacher of the deaf becomes the guide. Everyone who works with young deaf children agrees that early intervention is essential in terms of critical periods of learning and that the parent is very important in the early education program.

Historically, perhaps the best known parent program is the correspondence course of the John Tracy Clinic made available to mothers of deaf children in the United States and translated for use in some foreign countries. This gives parents specific procedures to develop sensory discrimination, imitation of movement, and improve muscle coordination. Parents found the correspondence course beneficial but some became discouraged because they could not understand the application to the learning of speech and lip reading skills. Guidance from a teacher of the deaf or opportunities to observe the instruction of deaf children would have been a great help.

Brief summer sessions lasting one or two weeks are offered to parents and preschool age deaf children at some of the state residential schools. In this period parents observe teaching, share in discussion groups, learn how to communicate with their deaf child and are prepared for the school program when their children enroll. A lot of information is crammed into this brief indoctrination session with little or no chance to practice under expert guidance.

All parents have opportunities in their homes for shaping linguistic and cognitive behavior. However, parents need help in translating what they are told to do into actually doing it in their own homes according to Simmons-Martin (1972).

One way to help mothers is through the services of an itinerant teacher who visits the home on a regular schedule. In this kind of program the teacher can observe the child in his home environment and meet his siblings.

Real situations in the child's life become opportunities to teach lip reading and language in a way that motivates the child to communicate. Mother can utilize a home experience and be guided immediately in making it meaningful to the child. This is an excellent program for the mother who cannot get a baby sitter for the siblings or one who lacks transportation, but she misses the chance to meet other mothers of deaf infants to compare experiences. Another disadvantage is the time required for the teacher to travel to the homes of the deaf children.

The Home Demonstration Center at Central Institute is in an old house with two apartments furnished as any average middle class home would be equipped. There are no offices, filing cabinets, or group hearing aids around. The mother can do any household chores she would do at home and talk to the deaf infant about them as she would talk to her hearing babies. She may bake cookies, wash dishes, make the bed, set the table, or just play with the child. The teacher is there to help the parents take advantage of every opportunity for language input. Good *mothering* techniques are reinforced. The mother has tasks planned for the hour and the teacher is ready to guide, encourage, and suggest procedures to develop the need for the child to communicate.

The Home Demonstration Center has great advantages because it conserves the time of the teachers, it protects the privacy of the parent's home, and it enables mothers of deaf children to meet. The teacher is not reluctant in the Demonstration Home to open closet doors, look in the refrigerator, and even make derogatory remarks about the dirty dishes in the sink!

Group education of the families is an essential part of the preschool education program. All of the family needs to get involved—fathers, grandparents, and older siblings. Large group meetings provide opportunities for the audiologist to talk about hearing aids; for the child psychologist to talk about child development and behavior problems; for the pediatrician to discuss health and immunizations; for the social worker to stress family and neighborhood relations; for the educator to prepare the parents for continued special education; for the adult deaf to describe their problems of adjustment to public schools, work, social life, and family.

Smaller groups should meet at least once a month with opportunities to discuss their own problems. This would include a father's meeting, a meeting of mothers just starting the program, and other groups of mothers who have been involved in the parent-infant program for one year or longer.

Northcott (1972) adds the PIP (Pop-in-Parent) to her program. As soon as a child is enrolled in the Minnesota Parent-Infant Program the parents are contacted by a PIP who explains the program and answers questions. An attempt is made to match the experienced parent with the new parent.

From the individual child centered program the infant moves into a small class two or three mornings a week and by the age of three to daily attendance. This gives an opportunity for socialization and time for more group discussion for mothers.

In some schools a trained nursery school teacher is in charge of the school program of nursery school activities and the deaf children receive individual speech and language therapy from the experienced teacher of the deaf. The danger of this kind of program lies in the failure of the teachers to coordinate the teaching. The nursery school group may be busy with finger-painting or other crafts, may be enjoying an active game, or may be sharing a mid-morning snack. The children are learning to attend to the activity, they are happy to be together, the aggressive ones learn to share, the isolate is drawn into the group, but there may be no attempt to encourage lip reading, vocalization, or imitation of a speech pattern. The speech tutor is not giving the language of the activity; or, if she is, the activity may be completed before the child joins the group and the need to communicate in the situation has been lost.

In some preschool classes the children remain with the teacher of the deaf throughout the session. She may be assisted by a teacher aide or a mother helper. It is recommended that children between the ages of three and five attend for one session only rather than the entire school day. The size of the class should not exceed seven if there is a helper.

In some school systems the length of time the child is in school is regulated by the bus or taxi schedule. Parents often equate hours in school with amount of academic progress. They need to be reminded that a deaf child is required to *work* a little harder than his hearing siblings in terms of attention and concentration and therefore, extra time in school must be spent in rest periods and play. It is therefore recommended that the preschoolage child attend classes for one session and the mother continue her part in the one-to-one relation at home, giving the child the language and the motivation to use it in his environment.

Simmons-Martin (1970) believes that when children have learned to make maximum use of their hearing and when the teacher takes on the role of mother models, hearing impaired children approach the stages linguists consider to be universal.

In preschool classes at Central Institute under the direction of Dr. Simmons-Martin, the children follow the stages of language development observed in the hearing child. The teacher must first provide a model for the child to imitate and then reinforce his first attempts at vocalization. The deaf child needs to know that he can manipulate people through his phonation.

The teacher must contrive situations and present the language in entire sentence form. The experiences should be appropriate for the child's age. Because the children and the teacher together have performed the activities, the linguistic form takes on meaning.

The language stories or experiences are written on charts with appropriate illustrations and the children like to review the activity and talk about it again and again.

Like hearing children, the deaf child responds and imitates affective patterns first. Feelings of surprise, happiness or dissatisfaction usually can be easily imitated. The teacher must be sensitive to what the child wishes to express and help him give vocal form to his feelings. The intonation of the sentences presented by the teacher stands the best chance of carrying meaning.

To get the child to attend to sounds he cannot hear, the sentences should be printed. Children are asked to match the *time envelope* of the teacher's model and in order to do this they must limit breath and articulatory movement.

Parents continue to be an important part of the child's communicative development. They are urged to visit class frequently. Teachers show mothers how to follow the topic the child initiates using short, simple sentences that include the structural words. It is very important that the child knows that his mother knows what he has learned in the classroom. Conferences of parent and teacher do not have the same impact on the child as his knowledge that mother was there and saw and heard him.

As the child continues in the preschool program and approaches primary levels, the school day lengthens, subjects of the curriculum are added, that is he learns to read and write, he learns some arithmetic and is introduced to science but all this is incorporated in lesson plans for language acquisition. Amplification through his aid gives him the teachers' model and he repeats, with strong reinforcement, especially when the information is initiated by the child. Attention to improved articulation begins and the child is eager to use better speech to express his ideas and to control his environment through his communication skills.

In today's evaluation of hearing impaired children, attention is directed toward the increase of congenital deafness over acquired deafness. Along with the increase in congenital deafness is the increase in children with multiple handicaps. Some of the multiple handicaps are attributed to maternal rubella and the *rubella child* frequently has a hearing impairment which may be accompanied by visual impairment, mental retardation, language learning and perceptual problems, or emotional disturbances. In his review of the deaf child in the '70's, Calvert (1970) warns that we should not overgeneralize expected behavioral characteristics based on a common etiology. The visual problem may be detected before the infant leaves the hospital, for example congenital cataract; the mental retardation is indicated at the time of evaluation by the mental test scores; but many of the other problems require diagnostic teaching. The skilled teacher must be aware that all deaf children do not acquire speech and lipreading skills at the same rate or in the same way. There is the possibility of a central nervous system deficit referred to by Myklebust (1964) as a psychoneurological learning disorder.

Parents and teachers must coordinate their efforts through the diagnostic teaching procedures. Is the emotional disturbance due to frustration from failure to communicate or does the emotional disturbance interfere with the acquisition of communication? Only skilled teaching and skilled parental management with infinite patience and love give an answer.

Does the child have a poor memory span for constantly changing successive stimuli such as lip movements? Should information concerning his environment be supplied in smaller units, should there be more frequent reinforcement? When should the teacher alter her approach? How should she advise the parent?

The multiply handicapped child presents a challenge and further complications to our preschool programs. Unfortunately no quick cookbook recipe has been found to meet the problem. The only answer seems to rest with the intuitive skills of the diagnostic teacher.

SUMMARY

1. Early identification of hearing loss is critical in the education of the deaf child. This is now possible through periodic testing of children on a High Risk Register.
2. Parents need help as soon as the diagnosis of deafness is confirmed. Parent guidance becomes the role of the counsellor.
3. A complete evaluation of the child including hearing tests, mental tests, case history information, observation of play and vocalizations of the child by an expert, is necessary in counselling the parents.
4. Parents of deaf children need to become involved in a Parent-Infant program to start education early. They have a right to select the kind of program they want and should have the privilege of visiting school programs to observe classes from preschool to graduation.
5. Early amplification is critical in the child's development starting with mother's voice close to his ear and continuing with the use of hearing aids worn throughout his waking hours but with ap-

propriate precautions for the infant, and sensible restrictions for the preschool age child (Example: do not wear the aid in the swimming pool).

6. The parent must always be involved in the language teaching process and cannot assume that classroom enrollment is a substitute for home teaching.

The hope for the deaf child to achieve his full potential lies in the availability of early education, the improvements in hearing testing and amplification, the involvement of parents, and the adequacy of teacher education. The success of a deaf adult, however we may define success, is usually the result of his personal motivation and the cooperative efforts of his parents combined with the skill and dedication of his teachers.

REFERENCES

Calvert, Donald R.: The Deaf Child in the Seventies. *Volta Rev, 72:*14-20, 1970.

Davis, Hallowell: The Young Deaf Child: Identification and Management. Proceedings of a Conference, Toronto, Canada. *Acta Oto-Laryngologica;* Stockholm, Supplementum 206, 1-21, 1965.

Hirsh, Ira: *Auditory Training. Hearing and Deafness.* Holt, Rinehart and Winston, 3rd Edition, Chap. 13, 346-359, 1970.

Hiskey-Nebraska Test of Learning Aptitude. Lincoln, Union College Press, 1966.

Levine, Edna: *Psychology of Deafness.* New York, Columbia Univ. Press, p. 126-137, 1960.

Mindel, Eugene and Vernon, McKay: *They Grow in Silence, the Deaf Child and His Family.* National Association for the Deaf, Silver Spring, Md. p. 17-22, 1971.

Myklebust, H.: Other Handicaps, *Psychology of Deafness.* New York, Grune & Stratton, p. 364-378, 1964.

Northcott, Winifred: *Developing Parent Participation.* Parent Programs in Child Development Centers. Lillie, David (Ed.), Univ. of No. Carolina, Chapel Hill, N. C. First Chance for Children, *1:*53-59, 1972.

Poull, Louise et al.: *The Randall's Island Performance Series.* New York, Columbia University Press, 1931.
Copyright purchased Central Institute for the Deaf, St. Louis, Mo. 1950.

Schlesinger, Hilde S. and Meadow, Kathryn P.: *Emotional Support to Parents.* Parent Programs in Child Development Centers. Lillie, David (Ed.), Univ. of No. Carolina, Chapel Hill, N. C., First Chance for Children, *1:*13-23, 1972.

Simmons, Audrey A.: *Language and Hearing. Speech for the Deaf Child.* Connor, Leo (Ed.), A. G. Bell Association for the Deaf, Washington, D. C., p. 280-292, 1971.

Simmons-Martin, Audrey A.: *Facilitating Parent-Child Interactions.* Parent Programs in Child Development Centers. Lillie, David (Ed.), Univ. of No. Carolina, Chapel Hill, N. C., First Chance for Children, *1*:43-50, 1972.

Smith, Alathena: *Performance of Subjects Aged Two to Four on Nonverbal Tasks Presented in Pantomime: A Phase in the Development of a Test for the Clinical Appraisal of Hypacousic and Other Language Handicapped Children.* Ph.D. Dissertation Ohio State University (1960), University of Michigan Microfilms, Inc. Mic. 60-6422.

Snijders, J. Th. and Snijders-Ooman, N.: *Non-Verbal Intelligence Tests for Deaf and Hearing Subjects.* Groningen, Holland, J. B. Wolters, 1959.

Thomas, Hoben: Psychological Assessment Instruments for Use With Human Infants. *Merrill-Palmer Quar 16*:176-223, 1970.

Chapter XI

PSYCHOLOGICAL ADJUSTMENT TO HEARING LOSS AND DEAFNESS

Brian Bolton, John G. Cull and Richard E. Hardy

The reader should be immediately aware that there is no such science, philosophy or discipline as a psychology of deafness. What is available in terms of understanding the psychology of deafness has come from the results of psychological and psychosocial studies of persons who have various types of hearing problems.

It is true that our clients are much more like us than unlike us, but they more than likely differ in one major respect. They have suffered the psychological impact of disability and have adjusted or are in the process of adjusting to this impact. In this chapter we shall discuss the factors which affect the psychological adjustment to deafness and the mechanisms through which individuals adjust.

During the first and second world wars, behavioral scientists noticed an increased incidence in conversion reactions. Conversion reactions are (APA, 1965) a type of psychoneurotic disorder in which the impulse causing anxiety is *converted* into functional symptoms in parts of the body rather than the anxiety being experienced consciously. Examples of conversion reactions include such functional disabilities as anesthesias (blindness, deafness), paralyses (aphonia, monoplegia, hemiplegia), and dyskineses (tic, tremor, catalepsy).

The study of these conditions along with other studies led to the development of a discipline known as psychosomatic medicine. Psychosomatic medicine is concerned with the study of the effects of the personality and emotional stresses upon the body and its function. This psychological interaction with physiology can be observed in any of the body systems.

After the establishment of psychosomatic medicine, behavioral scientists (psychiatrists, psychologists, social workers, etc.) began observing the converse of this new field. Instead of studying the effects of emotional stress on bodily functioning, they studied the effects of physical stress on emotional functioning. Their concern was directed toward answering the question, "What are the emotional and personality changes which result from physical stress or a change in body function or physical configuration?"

ROLE OF BODY IMAGE IN ADJUSTMENT

This new area of study became known as somatopsychology. The basis for this study is the body image concept. The body image is a complex conceptualization which we use to describe ourselves. It is one of the basic parts of the total personality and as such determines our reaction to our environment. According to English and English (1966) the body image is the mental representation one has of his own body.

There are two aspects of the body image concept—the ideal body image (the desired body image) and the actual body image. The greater the congruity between these two images the better the psychological adjustment of the individual, and conversely, the greater the discrepancy between these two parts of the self concept, the poorer an individual's psychological adjustment. This is very understandable. If an individual is quite short and views himself as such but has a strong ideal body image of a tall person, he is less well adjusted than he would be if his desired image were that of a short person.

In order to adjust to the psychological impact of deafness, the body image has to change from the image of a hearing person to the body image of an individual who does not hear or who has limited hearing. Early in the adjustment process the actual body image will change from that of a hearing person to the actual body image of a non-hearing person; however, for adequate psychological adjustment to deafness, the ideal body image must make the corresponding adaption. Therefore, in essence, psychological adjustment to disability is the acceptance of an altered body image which is more in harmony with reality.

FACTORS ASSOCIATED WITH ADJUSTMENT

There are three groups of factors which determine the speed or facility with which an individual will adjust to his disability. They help an individual understand the degree of psychological impact a particular disability is having on a client and the significance of his adjustment.

The first of these three groups of factors are those directly associated with the disability. Psychological effects of disabilities may arise from direct insult or damage to the central nervous system. These psychological effects are called brain syndromes and may be either acute or chronic. In this instance there are a variety of behavioral patterns which may result directly from the disability. In disabilities involving no damage to brain tissue the physical limitations imposed by the disability may cause excessive frustration and in turn result in behavioral disorders. For example, an active outdoorsman and nature lover may experience a greater psychological impact upon becoming deaf than an individual who leads a more restricted and physically limited life since the restrictions imposed by the disability demand a greater change in the basic life style for the first person. Therefore, factors directly associated with the disability have an important bearing upon an individual's reaction to disability.

The second group consists of those factors arising from the individual's attitude toward his disability. An individual's adjustment to his disability is dependent upon the attitudes he had prior to his disability. If his attitudes toward the deaf were quite negative and strong he will naturally have a greater adjustment problem than an individual with a neutral or positive attitude toward disability and the disabled, or specifically, the deaf and deafness. A part of this attitude formation prior to deafness is dependent upon the experiences the client has had with other deaf individuals and the stereotypes he has developed.

The amount of fear a client experiences or the emotion he expends during the onset and duration of the illness or accident leading up to the disability will determine the psychological impact of the disability. Generally, the greater the amount of emotion expended during onset the better the psychological adjustment to the disability. If an individual suddenly loses his hearing, his psychological reaction to the disability is much greater than if a great deal of emotion is expended during the process of losing hearing.

The more information an individual has relating to his disability the less impact the disability will have. If an individual who has recently lost his hearing is told about this loss in a simple, straightforward, mechanistic manner, he can much more easily accept and adjust to the disability than if the disability remains shrouded in a cloak of ignorance and mystery. The reader should keep in mind a relatively few individuals are deafened suddenly. About 90 per cent of the individuals who are rehabilitation clients are either born deaf or become so before the age of two. Any strangeness or unpredictable aspect of our body associated with its function immediately creates anxiety and if not clarified rapidly can result in totally debilitating anxiety. Therefore, it is important for psychological adjustment to a disability that the individual have communicated to him, in terms he can understand, the medical aspects of his disability as soon after onset of disability as possible.

When we are in strange or uncomfortable surroundings, our social perceptiveness becomes keener. Social cues which are below threshold or are not noticed in comfortable surroundings become highly significant to us in new, strange or uncomfortable surroundings. Upon the onset of deafness, the client will develop a heightened perceptiveness relative to how he is being treated by family, friends, and professionals. If others start treating him in a condescending fashion and relegate him to a position of less importance, his reaction to the psychological impact of the deafness will be poor. Professionals can react to the client from an anatomical orientation (what is missing) or a functional orientation (what is left). The anatomical orientation is efficient for classification purposes but is completely dehumanizing. The functional orientation is completely individualistic and as such enhances a client's adjustment to his disability.

Perhaps a key concept in the adjustment to deafness is the evaluation of the future and the individual's role in the future. In many physical medicine rehabilitation centers, a rehabilitation counselor is one of the first professionals to see the patient after the medical crisis has passed. The purpose of this approach is to facilitate the patient's psychological adjustment. If he feels there is a potential for his regaining his independence and security the psychological impact of the deafness will be lessened. While the counselor cannot engage in specific vocational counseling with the patient, he can discuss the depth of the vocational rehabilitation program and through these preliminary counseling sessions the counselor can help the person who has recently lost his hearing evaluate the roles he might play in the future.

The last factor which determines the adjustment process is based upon the individual's view of the purpose of his body and the relationship this view has with the type and extent of disability. The views individuals have of their body may be characterized as falling somewhere on a continuum. At one end of the continuum is the view that the body is a tool to accomplish work; it is a productive machine. At the other end is the view that the body is an esthetic stimulus to be enjoyed and provide pleasure for others. This latter concept is much the same as we have for sculpture and harks back to the philosophy of the ancient Greeks. Everyone falls somewhere on this continuum. To adequately predict the impact of a disability upon an individual, one has to locate the placement of the individual upon this continuum and then evaluate the disability in light of the individual's view of the function of this body.

As an example of the above principle, consider the cases in which a day laborer and film actress sustain the same disabling injury—a deep gash across the face. Obviously, when considering the disability in conjunction with the assumed placements of these two along the functional continuum, the psychological impact will be greater for the actress; since we have assumed the day laborer views his body almost completely as a tool to accomplish work and the disability has not impaired that function, the psychological impact of the disability upon him will be minimal. However, if the disability were changed (they both sustained severe injury to the abdomen resulting in the destruction of the musculature of the abdominal wall) the psychological impact would be reversed. In this case the actress would view her disability as minimal since it did not interfere with the esthetic value of her body, while the day laborer's disability would be overpowering since it had substantial effects upon the productive capacity of his body.

The most obvious conclusion to be drawn from the above three factors is that the degree of psychological impact is not correlated with the degree of disability. This statement is contrary to popular opinion; however, disability and its psychological impact constitute a highly personalized event. Many counselors fall into the trap of equating degree of disability with degree of psychological impact. If the psychological impact suffered by a client is much greater than that considered *normal,* the counselor will oftentimes become impatient with the client. It should be remembered that relatively superficial disabilities may have devastating psychological effects.

LANGUAGE, COMMUNICATION SKILLS, AND INTELLIGENCE

Language and Communication

The normal nondeaf child learns the language of the society into which he is born by hearing it. When auditory input is greatly reduced, language development in the child is effectively curtailed. Language refers to the verbal-graphic symbol system that is taken for granted by most people because it seems to occur naturally. In fact, language is man's greatest achievement and his unique defining characteristic. Language is the foundation upon which our vastly complex civilization is built. Culture is transmitted through the medium of language. Language is a tool which enables man to think abstractly, i.e., to construct and manipulate mental representations to solve problems (however, language is *not* the only basis for abstraction).

Communication refers to various signaling systems which exist or develop among animals, including man. The communication systems of most animals are innately determined and serve the sole function of continuing the survival of the species. (One theoretical position regarding language acquisition in man maintains that linguistic capacity is innate, too.) Thus, communication includes a much larger range of behaviors than language; however, language provides one (highly elaborate) procedure for communication among men.

The distinction between language and communication has direct relevance to the functioning of deaf persons. Most deaf persons are adequate communicators using manual sign *language,* but are extremely retarded in their use of formal language skills (reading and writing). Many authorities do not consider manual sign *language* to be a true language, but rather an advanced communication system. A longstanding controversy among deaf educators revolves around the relative merits of *oral* versus *manual* techniques of communication and language learning; the issues are summarized in the following section.

Language and Communication Training

Because deafness is synonymous with impaired language acquisition (Cull and Hardy, 1973) and reduced ability to communicate, language development and the training of communication skills have been the focus of educational programs for deaf children. Three basic approaches can be delineated: (1) the traditional oral method which stresses the skills of speech and speech reading, (2) the amplified hearing method which is premised on a developmental view of hearing, i.e., listening is a learned function, and (3) the *total communication* method which allows and encourages the use of fingerspelling and manual signs. Differences among these three approaches are, for the most part, a matter of degree, e.g., children trained under all three methods usually wear individual hearing aids; speech and speechreading skills are utilized by all three, but the degree of emphasis varies. Proponents of the three methods can cite evidence to support their favorite combination of techniques: Di Carlo (1964) writes convincingly of the traditional oral approach; Fry (1966) summarized arguments and presented data supporting the amplification approach; and Vernon and Koh (1970) reviewed and summarized a number of independent studies which favored the use of manual communication with deaf children. The only reasonable conclusion that can be reached at this time is that no method is appropriate for all deaf children. Furthermore, it is not possible to assign children to educational programs on the basis of hearing loss, intelligence, or any combination of characteristics. The importance of flexibility in the early language communication training of deaf children cannot be overemphasized.

Most professional rehabilitation workers with the deaf share a definite bias for the manual approach to communication. This bias reflects the belief that a viable communication system which allows deaf children and youth to interact with their peers and to learn the basic skills which constitute maturity is preferable to a poorly mastered formal language system. More specifically, the bias reflects the experience of rehabilitation personnel in attempting to habilitate twenty year old deaf adults who function socially as ten year olds. It is generally true that sign language restricts deaf persons to the deaf *subculture*, but this is viewed as the more desirable of the alternatives which are currently available. The issue is irrelevant anyway; most deaf persons associate with other deaf, join deaf social organizations, and intermarry.

Language and Intelligence

Most traditional theories of mental development have been premised on the central assumption that language is the primary vehicle of intellectual development. The assumption of interdependence of linguistic and intellectual development has been fundamental in psychology, e.g., Carmichael (1957) concluded that "In a most important sense, the development of language in an individual is the growth of a human mind in that person" (p. 193). The implication is that mental development is retarded or distorted in the absence of language. Investigations of the intellectual functioning of deaf subjects demonstrate that an individual's mental development is not dependent on the acquisition of language.

Investigations supporting the conclusion that intellectual development is independent of language development fall into three categories:

1. Comparative studies employing experimental learning tasks (Furth, 1964; 1966; 1971),
2. Comparative studies employing traditional (nonverbal) intelligence tests (Vernon, 1967; 1968), and
3. Correlational studies using intelligence tests and language communication assessments (Bolton, 1971a; 1971b; 1972).

The design of *comparative* studies is simple: matched samples of deaf and hearing subjects are compared on a variety of cognitive and perceptual tasks. Most comparative studies have concluded that there is no significant difference between deaf and hearing samples on learning tasks which do not require verbal mediation and, therefore, that language is not a necessary basis for abstract thinking and problem solving. Two points should be stressed: (1) many studies have found differences favoring hearing subjects, but these small differences reflect the cultural disadvantagement and lack of *testwiseness* that penalize any minority group on psychological tests, and (2) strictly speaking, the conclusion is debatable because almost all deaf persons possess some minimal language skills (Blank, 1965; Bornstein and Roy, 1973).

The design of *correlational* studies of deaf subjects also is simple; a fairly large sample is assessed on several measures of nonverbal intellectual functioning, language abilities, and communication skills. The intercorrelation matrix of variables is factor analyzed to obtain the major dimensions of the intelligence-language domain. The results of correlational studies support and strengthen the conclusion reached in comparative studies: measures of language abilities define factors separate from the nonverbal intelligence factors.

Communication Skills

The language communication abilities of deaf persons are three in number (Bolton, 1973): I. Manual Skills (manual signs and fingerspelling), II. Oral-Verbal Skills (speech and speechreading; reading and writing), and III. Residual Hearing. Strictly speaking, residual hearing is not a language communication modality. Furthermore, it is highly correlated with the development of oral communication skills (although it is only slightly related to measures of intelligence). A more important conclusion based on the results of several studies is that oral communication skills develop independently of manual communication skills and, therefore, that the early acquisition of manual skills does not impede the development of oral skills and may benefit linguistic development (see Bolton (1971a) and Vernon and Koh (1970) for a review of the research evidence).

PERSONALITY DEVELOPMENT AND SOCIAL ADJUSTMENT

It is generally recognized by child development specialists that a conception of selfhood becomes differentiated during the second or third year of life. The child's self concept forms in the context of the socialization processes, which are inextricably correlated with language training and development. A question of importance to psychologists and educators concerns the extent to which personality development and social adjustment of the young child may be distorted by retarded language development. In the following sections several topics related to this question are addressed and, where appropriate, conclusions are drawn.

Personality Assessment

In contrast to the relatively straight forward evaluation of intelligence, achievement, and special abilities, the assessment of personality development and social adjustment of profoundly deaf persons is a difficult task. Generally speaking, standard personality inventories are not applicable to deaf persons. In addition to requiring a reading level of approximately sixth grade, standard inventories contain items which are not appropriate for persons with hearing impairments. Many projective instruments (e.g., Rorschach, Thematic Apperception Test, etc.) are useful only with highly verbal deaf adults. Even with this small minority, the typical protocol is characterized by a paucity of responses with minimal elaboration. Most deaf adults lack the verbal facility to express their responses to unstructured stimuli. Finally, the traditional clinical interview relies to a great extent on verbal interchange between examiner and subject. When conducted by a psychologist fluent in manual sign language and experienced in work with deaf persons, the interview may provide useful information regarding personality functioning.

It is clear from the comments above that valid procedures for personality assessment of deaf children and adults are lacking. Therefore, all research studies are suspect and great caution must be exercised in interpreting results.

Personality Research

Six reviews of the research literature on personality and social adjustment of deaf and hard of hearing persons have been conducted during the last twenty years. Berlinsky (1952) reviewed fifteen studies and concluded (pp. 49 to 50) that deaf persons appear to reach about the same overall level of adjustment as the hearing population. He then proceeded to enumerate *some slight, but consistent differences.* Deaf persons have more trouble adjusting to their environment, they are more introverted, less dominant, slightly more neurotic, slightly more egocentric, evidence somewhat more feelings of depression and suspicion, and are less mature in judgment and social competence. Barker, et al. (1953) presented a more critical review of essentially the same studies. They refused to draw any conclusions about personality or adjustment of deaf adults due to inadequacy of the studies (p. 33). They concluded that deaf children in residential schools are more poorly adjusted, more unstable emotionally, and more neurotic than children with normal hearing (p. 33). Di Carlo and Dolphin (1952) reviewed more than a dozen studies of the personality and social adjustment of deaf children and adults and concluded that the results were inconclusive. They were especially critical of research design and measurement procedures employed in the studies. Meyerson (1963) considered the available studies of personality and social adjustment of deaf children and concluded that ". . . deafness is not directly related to personality in the sense that it requires a particular kind of adjustment" (p. 143). Levine (1963) reviewed a wide variety of studies and concluded that "the personality patterns and traits of the deaf suggest weakness and deficiencies for dealing effectively and knowledgeably with the complex problems of life today" (p. 508). The final review by Schuldt and Schuldt (1972) considered twenty empirical personality studies of deaf children published since 1950. They concluded that deaf children manifest more abnormal personality characteristics and less adequate adjustment when compared to hearing children.

The reviewers are clearly not in agreement in their conclusions regarding the personality and adjustment of deaf persons. This may be due to several factors, not the least of which is the diversity of methods and inconsistent results of the various studies. It is important to point out that all reviewers advised caution in interpreting their conclusions as indicating maladjustment or psychopathology. The question of practical concern remains: "What reasonable conclusion can be drawn from the currently available studies of the personality and social adjustment of deaf children and adults?" If it is assumed that ". . . what is normal or realistic for a hearing person may not be realistic for an individual who has impaired hearing" (Myklebust, 1964, p. 158), then the only defensible conclusion is similar to Levine's (1963) noted previously. Many deaf adults are deficient in the common knowledge and basic social skills that the average hearing person takes for granted. Most deaf persons grow up in a restricted environment and consequently they exhibit retarded behavior patterns. Generally speaking, these characteristics and conditions are responsive to educational, rehabilitative treatments as contrasted to psychological or psychiatric intervention.

Organismic Shift Hypothesis

Many psychologists have hypothesized that any sensory deprivation produces an alteration of the pattern of sensory integration and subsequent modification of behavior. Myklebust has been the foremost proponent of this notion in the study of the psychological effects of deafness. His *organismic shift hypothesis* is best stated by him:

> "A sensory deprivation limits the world of experience. It deprives the organism of some of the material resources from which the mind develops. Because total experience is reduced, there is an imposition on the balance and equilibrium of all psychological processes. When one type of sensation is lacking, it alters the integration and function of all of the others. Experience is now constituted differently; the world of perception, conception, imagination, and thought has an altered foundation, a new configuration (1964, p. 1)."

Myklebust's explanation of the impact of organismic shift on the personality development of deaf children relies to a great extent on an intermediate cause, that of language deprivation. Again, in Myklebust's words:

> "There is an assumption that deafness alters experience, that it causes an imposition on monitoring, and that it forces detachment and isolation. Furthermore, language is viewed as a significant factor in the development of personal-social contacts and interaction. Language is assumed to be the primary means whereby experience is internalized, crystallized, and structured. Hence, when language is limited there might be a reciprocal restriction in ability to integrate experience; the personality might be less structured, more immature, less subtle, and more sensorimotor in character (1964, pp. 118-119)."

There is no argument regarding the observation that many deaf youth and adults do exhibit retarded emotional development and personal functioning. What is disputed is the nature of the hypothesized cause; a much simpler explanation holds that deficits in experience are responsible for retarded personal, social functioning. The organismic shift hypothesis requires more confirming evidence before it can attain the status of an explanatory mechanism in the psychology of deafness.

ABILITIES, INTERESTS, AND ATTITUDES

Special Abilities

Nonverbal abilities can be divided into two classes: (1) those which emerge primarily as a function of the maturational processes (e.g., spatial, clerical, and psychomotor abilities) and (2) those which require special training, or exposure to certain activities, and/or extended practice to stimulate optimal development (e.g., mechanical, artistic, and mathematical abilities). Deaf persons possess abilities of the first type in the same degree as hearing persons, but they often do not acquire the requisite experiences to develop abilities of the second type. The psychologist who evaluates deaf clients should be careful to distinguish between tests which measure *natural* abilities and those which reflect learning experiences.

Interests

Interests develop in response to environmental stimulation and opportunities. Unlike abilities, the concept of interest requires an object of attention; interests do not exist apart from experience, which may be either vicarious or real. Because deaf persons are often not exposed to a wide range of educational and cultural experiences, their interests may be accurately described as underdeveloped. Thus, the measurement of interest patterns of deaf persons presents problems. Standard inventories such as the Strong and Kuder assume knowledge of activities which most deaf persons do not have. One of the several pictorial inventories which have been constructed, the Geist Picture Interest Inventory, was designed especially for use with deaf subjects. It has been demonstrated to be psychometrically deficient and clinically useless. Vocational guidance of deaf youth would be greatly improved by the development of a valid measure of interests.

Attitudes

Two aspects of attitude toward deafness may be delineated: (1) the actual attitudes held by hearing persons, and (2) the attitudes that deaf persons believe that hearing persons hold (perceived attitudes). Both aspects of attitude toward deafness are potentially detrimental to deaf people: actual attitudes may result in real barriers to education, employment, etc., while perceived attitudes influence the deaf person's motivation and estimate of self worth. The available evidence indicates that deaf persons devalue deafness more than hearing persons and that they believe that hearing people hold more negative attitudes toward deafness than they actually do. These conclusions have clear implications for educators of deaf children and youth, as well as rehabilitation counselors working with deaf adults. The interested reader is referred to Schroedel and Schiff (1972) for a review of the research evidence.

ROLE OF DEFENSE MECHANISMS IN ADJUSTMENT

While the three groups of factors discussed above determine the length of time required for adjustment to hearing loss, the path to adjustment is best described by defense mechanisms. Defense mechanisms are psychological devices used by all to distort reality. Often reality is so harsh it is unacceptable to us. Therefore, we distort the situation to make it more acceptable. Defense mechanisms are used to satisfy motives which cannot be met in reality; they reduce tensions in personal interactions; and they are used to resolve conflicts. To be effective they must be unconscious. They are not acquired consciously or deliberately. If they become conscious they become ineffective as defenses and others must replace them. For the major part of the remainder of this chapter we will look at the defenses most often employed by the disabled in the general order of their use.

Denial

Denial is an unconscious rejection of an obvious fact which is too disruptive of the personality or too emotionally painful to accept. Therefore, in order to soften reality the obvious fact is denied. Immediately upon onset of disability the individual denies it happened. Then, as the fact of the disability becomes so overwhelming its existence can no longer be denied, there is a denial of the permanency of the disability. The individual who has recently lost hearing, while utilizing the defense of denial, will adamantly maintain that he will be able to hear again. There will be a miraculous cure or a new surgical technique will be discovered.

While there are few steadfast rules in human behavior, one is that rehabilitation at best can be only marginally successful at this point. Rehabilitation cannot proceed adequately until the client accepts the permanency of the disability and is ready to cope with the condition. This is what is meant by many professionals when they say a client must accept his hearing loss. Most clients have real difficulty accepting severe hearing loss, but they should and will accept the permanence of the loss.

Withdrawal

Withdrawal is a mechanism which is used to reduce tension by reducing the requirements for interaction with others within the individual's environment. There are two dynamics which result from withdrawal. In order to keep from being forced to face the acceptance of hearing loss, the individual withdraws (as a result of his changed physical condition) and his social interaction is quite naturally reduced. His circle of interest as determined by friends, business, social responsibilities, church, civic responsibilities and family is drastically reduced. Thus, he becomes egocentrically oriented until finally his entire world revolves around himself.

Rather than functioning interdependently with his environment to mutually fulfill needs as our culture demands, he is concerned exclusively with his environment fulfilling his needs. As his world becomes more narrowed, his thoughts and preoccupations become more somatic. Physiological processes heretofore unconscious now become conscious. At this point he begins using another defense mechanism—regression.

Regression

Regression is the defense mechanism which reduces stress by avoiding it. The individual psychologically returns to an earlier age that was more satisfying. He adopts the type of behavior that was effective at that age but now has been outgrown and substituted by more mature behavior—behavior which is more effective in coping with stressful situations.

As the individual with a recent hearing loss withdraws, becomes egocentric, and hypochrondriacal, he will regress to an earlier age which was more satisfactory. This regression may be manifested in two manners. First he may, in his regression, adopt the dress, mannerisms, speech, etc. of contemporaries at the age level to which he is regressing. Secondly, he may adopt the outmoded dress, mannerisms, speech, etc. of the age to which he regressed. This second manifestation of regression is considerably more maladaptive since it holds the individual out to more ridicule which, at this point in his adjustment to his deafness, quite possibly will result in more emphasis on the defense mechanism of withdrawal.

While utilizing the first three defense mechanisms, if reality is being harshly pushed on him and his defenses are not working, he may as a last resort become highly negative of those around him and negative in general. This negativism is demonstrated as an active refusal, stubbornness, contradictory attitudes and rebellion against external demands. He may become abusive of those around and may become destructive in an effort to act out the thwarting he is experiencing. This negativistic behavior is an indication that the defense mechanisms he is employing are not distorting reality enough to allow him to adjust to his newly acquired disabled status. If, however, he is able to adjust and the defense mechanisms are effective to this point, he will employ the next defense.

Repression

Repression is selective forgetting. It is contrasted with suppression which is a conscious, voluntary forgetting. Repression is unconscious. Events are repressed because they are psychologically traumatic. As mentioned above the attitudes the client had relative to deafness and the deaf has a major bearing upon his adjustment. If these attitudes are highly negative the client will have to repress them at this point if his adjustment is to progress. Until he represses them he will be unable to accept the required new body image.

Reaction Formation

When an individual has an attitude which creates a great deal of guilt, tension, or anxiety and he unconsciously adopts the opposite of this attitude, he has developed a reaction formation. In order to inhibit a tendency to flee in terror a boy will express his nonchalance by whistling in the dark. Some timid persons, who feel anxious in relating with others, hide behind a facade of gruffness and assume an attitude of hostility to protect themselves from fear. A third and last example is that of a mother who, feeling guilty about her rejection of a newborn child, may adopt an attitude of extreme overprotectiveness to reduce the anxiety produced by this guilt of rejection. This example is seen more often in cases of parents with handicapped children.

In this new, dependent role the individual who has lost his hearing will feel a varying degree of hostility and resentment toward those on whom he is so dependent—wife, relatives, etc. Since these feelings are unacceptable he will develop a reaction formation. The manifest behavior will be marked by concern, love, affection, closeness—all to an excessive degree.

Fantasy

Fantasy is daydreaming. It is the imaginary representative of satisfactions that are not attained in real experience. This defense mechanism quite often accompanies withdrawal. As the client starts to adjust to a new body image and a new role in life, he will develop a rich, overactive fantasy life. In this dreamworld he will place himself into many different situations to see how well he fits.

Rationalization

Rationalization is giving socially acceptable reasons for behavior and decisions. There are four generally accepted types of rationalization. The first is called blaming an incidental cause: the child who stumbles blames the stool by kicking it; the poor or sloppy workman blames his tools. Sour grapes rationalization is called into play when an individual is thwarted. A goal to which the individual aspires is blocked to him; therefore, he devalues the goal by saying he did not really want it so much. The opposite type of rationalization is called sweet lemons. When something the individual does not want is forced upon him, he will modify his attitude by saying it was really a very desirable goal and he feels quite positive about the new condition. The fourth and last type of rationalization is called the doctrine of balances. In this type of rationalization we balance positive attributes in others with perceived negative qualities. And conversely, we balance negative attributes with positive qualities. For example, beautiful women are assumed to be dumb, bright young boys are assumed to be weak and asthenic and the poor are happier than the rich.

The deaf individual will have to rationalize his disability in order to assist himself in accepting the permanence of the deafness. One rationalization may be that he had nothing to do with his current condition, but that something over which he had no control caused the deafness. Another dynamic which might be observed is the adherence to the belief on the part of the client that as a result of the deafness there will be compensating factors. He will develop in other areas such as additional senses or aptitudes and talents he previously did not possess.

We once had a client whose rationalization of his disability ran something like this: All of the men in his family had been highly active outdoors types. They all had died prematurely with coronaries. He, the client, was a highly active outdoors type; however, now that he was severely disabled he would be considerably restricted in his activities. Therefore, he would not die prematurely. This logic resulted in the conclusion that the disability was positive and he was pleased he had become disabled. Granted, rationalization is seldom carried to this extreme in the adjustment to deafness, but this case is illustrative of a type of thinking which must occur for good adjustment.

Projection

A person who perceives traits or qualities in himself which are unacceptable may deny these traits and project them to others. In doing so he is using the defense mechanism of projection. A person who is quite stingy sees others as being essentially more stingy. A person who is basically dishonest sees others as trying to steal from him. A person who feels inferior rejects this idea and instead projects it to others; i.e., he is capable but others will not give him a chance because they doubt his ability. These are examples of projection. With the deaf person many of the feelings he has of himself are unacceptable. Therefore, in order to adjust adequately, he projects these feelings to society in general. *They* feel he is inadequate. *They* feel he is not capable. *They* feel he is inferior and is to be devalued. This type of thinking, normally, leads directly into identification and compensation which are in reality the natural exits to this maze in which he has been wandering around.

Identification

The defense mechanism of identification is used to reduce an individual's conflict through the achievement of another person or a group of people. Identification can be with material possessions as well as people. A person may derive his social adequacy and psychological adequacy through his clothes *(The clothes make the man),* his sports car, his hi-fi stereo paraphernalia, etc. People identify with larger groups in order to take on the power, prestige, and respect attributed to that organization *(our team won).* This larger group may be a club, lodge, garden club, college, professional group, etc.

In adjustment to his deafness, the client will identify with a larger group. It may be a group of other deaf persons, an occupational group, a men's lodge, a veterans' group, etc. But at this point in the adjustment process, he will identify with some group in order to offset some of the feelings he has as a result of the projection he is engaging in. If successful, the identification obviates the need to employ the mechanisms of denial, withdrawal, and regression.

Compensation

If an individual's path to a set of goals is blocked and he finds other routes to achieve that set of goals, he is using the defense mechanism of compensation. A teenager is seeking recognition and acceptance from his peers. He decides to gain this recognition through sports. However, when he fails to make the team he decides to become a scholar. This is an example of compensation. Compensation brings success; therefore, it diverts attention from shortcomings and defects, thereby eliminating expressed or implied criticism. This defense mechanism is most often used to reduce self criticism rather than external criticism. As the individual experiences successes he will become less preoccupied with anxieties relating to his disability and his lack of productivity.

Identification and compensation usually go together in the adjustment process. When the client starts using these two defenses he is at a point at which he may adequately adjust to the new body image and his new role in life.

SUMMARY

When a psychologist is dealing with a physical handicap, he always thinks about the differences in terms of psychological damage that physical handicaps cause various people. In other words, the handicap is always something of a highly individual nature. We are pretty much decided that there is no single factor which in and of itself can be used in the prediction of adjustment to a physical disability. This does not include, of course, such injury that would come about as a result of catastrophic trauma to the central nervous system of a progressive nature.

Anyone trying to ascertain and evaluate psychological reaction to physical disability must keep in mind: 1) that it is an individual reaction in every case; 2) the nature and extent of physical damage offers some information in that the less physically or mentally encompassing are the physiology reactions, the smaller is the probability of psychological handicaps; 3) generally speaking the age of the individual is of importance in terms of the seriousness of the psychological adjustment problem. If an individual has been born deaf, deafness surely presents a most basic set of influencing factors concerning his developing personality. If he suddenly loses hearing as a growing child, he must suffer sudden shock as a result of that disability. The child then who is born deaf may escape the trauma of losing his hearing but may then be faced with the problems of overprotection and dependence in reference to parents and family members. If an individual slowly begins to lose hearing in older age, this simply reinforces in him the fact that he is growing older and may cause him to have some severe questioning of his capability as well as presenting self concept problems, 4) the manner of onset also is a factor determining psychological reaction to physical disability as has just been explained. If the disability is sudden the individual has had no opportunity to prepare himself for it. If the disability is gradual, the individual has more opportunity to prepare himself for it but must face the concept of himself as a deteriorating individual physically.

Another (fifth) factor which always influences adjustment has to do with the attitudes of those individuals in support capabilities around the individual and his resources for overcoming the particular difficulty involved. The attitudes of both family and friends will have a great impact and can offer much to the individual or hinder him substantially in his adjustment process.

The next factor (sixth) has to do with the beginning of a rehabilitation effort which is somewhat organized for the individual. The longer period of time which goes by the more the person's pattern of inadequate adaptation can become permanent. After some period of time it may be difficult for him to show much responsiveness to the rehabilitation effort. Any individual who is suddenly traumatized by a physical disability of a permanent nature will need a period of grief and mourning before he can begin any real constructive rehabilitation period. The periods vary with individuals and counselors will have to make individual decisions concerning whether the person needs a matter of a few days or several weeks or a month or two in order to readjust his concept of self and evaluate fully the challenge which is before him.

The individual suddenly disabled with severe physical problems such as deafness experiences a life environment which seems highly closed and his entire psychic structure is shaken. His understanding of himself in terms of his self concept, his psychic identity and his interaction and relationship with others including his immediate family, friends, and individuals in his work environment are all jeopardized. The individual who is profoundly deafened finds himself in a soundless world—a world which provides him nothing any longer in terms of cues or clues relating to what is going on around him.

No rehabilitation effort can be even partially successful without the active self participation of the individual himself. His family and close associates most often need to be brought in on establishing goals and determining reasonable progress towards these goals. We all see ourselves to a great extent in the eyes of others. The newly deafened individual is no exception; at no other time in his life will family and friends be more important to him.

IMPLICATIONS FOR PROFESSIONALS WORKING WITH THE DEAF

Almost everyone in our society views handicapping and disabling conditions from an anatomical point of view rather than functionally. It is imperative that the individual with a recent hearing loss be helped to view his disability functionally rather than anatomically. The client should gain an appreciation for the abilities he has left rather than classifying himself with a group based solely upon an anatomical loss.

The worker with the deaf should make sure the information which the client has is factual, concise, and clear. He should be sure the client's perception of his disability is correct and the cause is completely understood. This understanding greatly enhances the adjustment of the client to his deafness.

The deaf person should be helped in exploring his feelings regarding the manner in which he is currently being treated by family and friends. Help him to understand the natural emotional reactions he will have resulting from his newly acquired deafness; and help him to understand that the feelings of family and friends are going to be different for a period of time while they adjust to his disability.

The counselor should not fall into the trap of thinking that the degree of deafness is absolutely positively correlated with the degree of psychological impact. It must be realized that each individual's disability is unique unto that individual and his reaction to his disability will be unique.

Lastly, in summary, the most important role anyone can play in assisting a client in the adjustment to deafness is to be a warm, emphatic, accepting individual who is positive in his regard toward the client and who is pragmatic in counseling and planning efforts with the client.

REFERENCES

American Psychiatric Association: *Diagnostic and Statistical Manual of Mental Disorders.* Washington, D. C., American Psychiatric Association, 1965.

Barker, et al.: *Adjustment to Physical Handicap and Illness: A Survey of Physique and Disability.* Rev. Ed. New York, Social Science Research Council, 1953.

Berlinsky, S.: Measurement of intelligence and personality of the deaf: A review of the literature. *J Speech Hear Disord, 17:*39-54, 1952.

Blank, M.: The use of the deaf in language studies: A reply to Furth. *Psychological Bull, 63:*442-444, 1965.

Bolton, B. A factor analytic study of communication skills and nonverbal abilities of deaf rehabilitation clients. *Multivariate Behavioral Research, 6:*485-501, 1971. (a)

Bolton, B.: *Factor analytic studies of communication skills, intelligence, and other psychological abilities of young deaf persons.* Paper presented at the Psychometric Society meeting in St. Louis, Missouri, on April 8, 1971. (b)

Bolton, B.: *Factorial studies of communication skills, nonverbal intelligence, and other psychological abilities of deaf young adults:* Validation and refinement. Paper presented at the Southwestern Psychological Association meeting in Oklahoma City on April 21, 1972.

Bolton, B. An alternative solution for the factor analysis of communication skills and nonverbal abilities of deaf clients. *Educational and Psychological Measurement, 33:*459-463, 1973.

Bornstein, H. and Roy, H.: Comment on linguistic deficiency and thinking: Research with deaf subjects 1964-1969. *Psychological Bull, 79:*211-214, 1973.

Carmichael, L.: *Basic Psychology.* New York, Random House, 1957.

Cull, J. G. and Hardy, R. E.: Language meaning (gender shaping) among deaf and hearing students. *Perceptual and Motor Skills,* 1973, 36, 98.

Di Carlo, L. M.: *The Deaf.* Englewood Cliffs, Prentice-Hall, 1964.

Di Carlo, L. M. and Dolphin, J. E.: Social adjustment and personality development of deaf children: A review of the literature. *Exceptional Children, 8:*111-118, 1952. Reprinted in E. P. Trapp and P. Himelstein

(Eds.): *Readings on the Exceptional Child.* New York: Appleton-Century-Crofts, 1962.

English, H. B. and English, A. C.: *A Comprehensive Dictionary of Psychological and Psychoanalytical Terms.* New York, McKay, 1966.

Fry, D. B.: The development of the phonological system in the normal and the deaf child. In Smith, F. and Miller, G. A.: *The Genesis of Language: A Psycholinguistic Approach.* Cambridge, The MIT Press, 1966.

Furth, H. G.: Research with the deaf: Implications for language and cognition. *Psychological Bull, 62:*145-164, 1964.

Furth, H. G.: *Thinking Without Language.* New York: The Free Press, 1966.

Furth, H. G.: Linguistic deficiency and thinking: Research with deaf subjects, 1964-1969. *Psychological Bull, 76:*58-76, 1971.

Levine, E. S.: Studies in psychological evaluation of the deaf. *Volta Rev, 65:*496-512, 1963.

Meyerson, L.: A psychology of impaired hearing. In Cruickshank, W. M. (Ed.) *Psychology of Exceptional Children and Youth* (Second Ed.), 1963.

Myklebust, H. R.: *The Psychology of Deafness* (Rev. Ed.). New York, Grune & Stratton, 1964.

Schroedel, J. G. and Schiff, W.: Attitudes toward deafness among several deaf and hearing populations. *Rehabil Psychol, 19:*59-70, 1972.

Schuldt, W. J. and Schuldt, D. A.: A review of recent personality research on deaf children. In E. P. Trapp and P. Himelstein (Eds.): *Readings on the Exceptional Child* (Rev. Ed.). New York: Appleton-Century-Crofts, 1972.

Vernon, M.: Relationship of language to the thinking process. *Arch Gen Psych, 16:*325-333, 1967.

Vernon, M. and Koh, S. D.: Effects of early manual communication on achievement of deaf children. *Am Ann Deaf, 115:*527-536, 1970.

Chapter XII

HISTORY, ROLE, AND FUNCTION OF THE NATIONAL ASSOCIATION OF THE DEAF (NAD)

ROBERT O. LANKENAU

EARLY DAYS

FOR ALMOST NINETY YEARS the N.A.D. struggled to exist against seemingly overwhelming odds and only during the past eight years or so has it emerged as the organization it was meant to be and began to take an active role in the lives of deaf people all over the United States.

Up to the year 1960 the N.A.D. met every two years in cities and states that the membership voted on during the previous conventions and officers were elected for terms of four years by members in attendance at each convention. The financial structure was so precarious that only one or two employees could be hired to attend to the details of a national organization—in addition, the president put in countless hours at very little compensation. It was a hit and/or miss sort of *set-up* that never was able to get off the ground.

In 1960, during the Dallas Convention, Mr. David Wilson, a hearing man and staunch supporter of the N.A.D., suggested a sort of *cooperating plan* in which all state associations become affiliated with the N.A.D., pay a quota per regular member and be assigned representatives and voting rights in proportion to the number of members.

With this plan, we would for the first time be organized, have representation and, hopefully, induce *all* state associations to join.

It was not too difficult to get most of the various state associations to join. However, it required some persistent effort and patience to get all of them in our fold. It also took some special legislation to take care of those states with unique constitutions and by-laws. To date all but one state association is a member and at this printing it may already be a part of our organization.

In 1964 our convention was held in the Shoreham Hotel in Washington, D. C., and during that meeting we voted to move the home office from California (where it had been for eighteen years) to Washington, D. C. This motion to move originated from a proposal from the Wisconsin Association of the Deaf and was actually made at the 1962 Convention but personnel was unavailable until 1964.

Along with the move came a new slate of officers and things began to roll under the presidency of Robert G. Sanderson.

The actual move to Washington took place in September, 1964 and by October, 1964 our new offices were located at 2025 Eye Street, North West, in Suite 311. It consisted of two rooms.

Service Organization Advances

After moving was complete, the concept of the N.A.D. as a service organization began to take effect and one of the first projects was to cooperate with the Deafness Research Foundation in connection with the Temporal Bone Bank's Program. Following this, we set up a program to evaluate general entertainment films for Captioned Films for the Deaf, a department of the United States Office of Education.

Another major change was our policy regarding our official publication. The new administration decided to change the name from *Silent Worker* to *The Deaf American* and abandoned its long held concept that the magazine must be self supporting and instead insisted that the publication must be the N.A.D.'s *advance guard,* its *voice* to the state cooperating associations, and no expense be spared (within limits of the association's finances) to make this publication as informative and as attractive as possible. Circulation in 1964 was 2,400. By 1968 it grew to 3,700 and by 1972, after the administration of President Lankenau, it had grown to over 6,000 and is still growing.

At the 1966 Convention in San Francisco a decision was made to hire a full time executive secretary and Mr. Frederick Schreiber, then Secretary-Treasurer resigned to accept this appointment.

In July, 1967 the N.A.D. Home Office doubled its size and consisted of seven rooms with approximately 1,600 sq. feet of floor space. Additional clerical help was hired and as a result of the Registry of Interpreters for the Deaf Workshop held prior to the 1966 Convention which requested the N.A.D. to obtain governmental support in setting up a full time office and having an executive director for this, it was done in August, 1967.

By September, 1967 the N.A.D. Board was actively seeking applications for the director of its Manual Communications Program. In January, 1968 a director was appointed and the post was filled. This resulted in a need for a larger staff, so more help was hired.

From then on the N.A.D. began to acquire various pieces of new office equipment in order to reprint much of its outdated pamphlet file and to better be able to undertake the role of dissemination of information on the deaf to serve the hearing public.

The N.A.D. is a member of the President's Committee on the Employment of the Handicapped and has taken an active part in providing this group with help and advice as to the problems of deafness.

We have appeared before several congressional committees in support of various pieces of legislation that affect the deaf and we were active in supporting the founding of the National Technical Institute for the Deaf in Rochester, New York. This is now a part of Rochester Institute of Technology and a multimillion dollar complex is being built on their new campus to take care of the programs for the deaf.

We also supported the Model Secondary School program and the National Center for Deaf and Blind Youths and Adults.

Efforts have been directed at the creation of improved telephone communication in conjunction with American Telephone and Telegraph Company and other companies, in order to provide the necessary equipment at reasonable prices so that deaf people may now make use of ordinary telephones to communicate with each other.

We have made an effort to have a closer relationship with the National Association of Hearing and Speech Agencies and this has resulted in setting up community service agencies that help not only the hard of hearing but the profoundly deaf as well. To be exact we are working together toward common goals.

Our Junior N.A.D. program is touching the lives of deaf youth in all walks of life. It is bringing out hidden talents which never were known to exist and the result has been keen competition in various forms of individual cultural talent. We now have programs on local, state, regional and national levels. The winners in various categories compete against one another every two years at our convention.

The N.A.D. has undertaken the National Census of deaf people, with support from the Social and Rehabilitation Services of the Department of Health, Education, and Welfare. This census, the first in more than forty years, will be completed in mid-1973. While it will not include all deaf people because its criteria limits it to persons whose hearing loss occurred before the age of nineteen, it will provide not only numerical data but also the characteristics of the target group. It will be a reliable base on which improved educational, vocational, and social programs for the deaf can be built.

The N.A.D. has a grant which will bring the World Congress of the Deaf here to America in 1975. This organization tries to cope with the problems of deafness on an international basis, and it plays a growing responsibility in improving the overall position of the deaf educationally, vocationally, and socially all over the world.

The N.A.D. publishes books and sells various types of books related to deafness, its problems and the teaching of the language of signs. This new activity of selling books has resulted in an increased income for our association and serves as another source of steady income to continue our work. Among the books published and/or sold are: *A Dictionary of Idioms for the*

Deaf; They Grow in Silence; The Deaf Child and His Family; A Basic Course in Manual Communication; Say It With Hands; Ameslan (American Sign Language) as well as *Signing Exact English,* etc.

We try to go to the aid of our cooperating state associations when some local problem develops which could make use of experience we have had in other states of the same nature.

The National Association of the Deaf now employs twenty-three people and just recently purchased a $650,000 Home Office building at 814 Thayer Avenue, Silver Spring, Maryland. The top floor is devoted to N.A.D. work while the other two floors are rented out for rental income.

This national association was founded in 1880 in Cincinnati, Ohio and its first president was Robert P. McGregor of Ohio. He was a school teacher and a most effective orator using the language of signs. For many years he taught at the Ohio School for the Deaf in Columbus, Ohio.

Soon we will be making plans to celebrate our 100th anniversary and at this time it will be interesting to stop and take note of what the N.A.D. has accomplished to date and what it intends to accomplish in the next one hundred years.

It has helped many schools in combating the excessive use of oral methods of educating the deaf children. The N.A.D. believes that the oral method has a place in educating the hearing impaired but it is not the answer to a complete education in every respect. Individuals differ and the method of teaching them will differ. We believe in the *total communication* approach in which the teacher makes use of all reasonable methods of communication to teach our deaf children.

The N.A.D. furnishes information to college students who need specific answers to questions on deafness and problems associated with it. We also provide for our members information on the status of pending legislation either directly or indirectly affecting their lives and interpretative reports on both pending and existing laws.

The N.A.D. is in a continual battle to create a favorable social image of the deaf and it is deeply concerned about this. We believe that a deaf person should not be denied an opportunity to do a certain type of work until it has been proven without doubt he can not do it. Obviously, there are some things a deaf person just cannot do but even these are beginning to be overcome with the help of new inventions, new ideas, etc. The N.A.D. is strongly opposed to imposters and to hearing impaired who use sympathy to obtain *hand-outs* from the gullible public.

All in all, the N.A.D. tries to protect the basic rights of all deaf people, such as the privilege to drive a car and purchase insurance, the right to work for the United States Government, industry and other places providing he is capable, willing and deafness itself does not have a bearing on the job itself.

INDEX

D

E